# BEY
# THE TRIDENT

## A Navy SEAL's Search Through Trauma for Meaning in Life

A MEMOIR

TOM MURPHY

AUSTIN, TEXAS

**BEYOND THE TRIDENT**

A Navy SEAL's Search Through Trauma for Meaning in Life



Published by:
Self-published by Author.
Austin, Texas



Printed in the United States of America.
ISBN 9798878533171



The information in this book is not intended as a substitute for care from a licensed medical or mental health professional. If you are suffering from the effects of PTSD or other trauma, please seek the guidance and support you need.

Editing: Susan Priddy (SusanPriddy.com)

**Library of Congress Control Number**: TXu-2-418-254
Available in Paperback and Kindle

**Author: Tom Murphy**

# DEDICATION

To friends who said if I'd write it, they'd read it.

To combat veterans and all trauma sufferers worldwide.

To my love Heather, my sister Sharon, and my entire extended family for their lifelong love and support.

# ACKNOWLEDGMENTS

First and foremost, I want to extend the most heart-felt thanks to the spiritual teachers whose works and ideas have blessed and inspired me to try to help others find their personal spiritual paths.

I'd also like to thank everyone who helped me with professional and personal comments, edits, and assistance with the manuscript drafts. From my perspective, it took a village to write this book.

And a special "thank you" to my final editor, Susan Priddy, who was unfailingly good-humored and patient with me while she took the composite efforts of everyone who helped me with the manuscript and proceeded to "take it apart," and then put it into a better tone and format under the euphemism of "re-slicing the pie." My advice to anyone writing their first book would be, when you think you're finally done, locate someone like Susan.

## Dropping Keys [1]

*The small man*
*Builds cages for everyone*
*He*
*Knows,*
*While the sage,*
*Who has to duck his head*
*When the moon is low,*
*Keeps dropping keys all night long*
*For the*
*Beautiful*
*Rowdy*
*Prisoners*
**—Hafiz/*The Gift***

**Note:**

1. Hafiz, a Persian mystic and Sufi poet, wrote these poems almost a thousand years ago. Hafiz is believed to have written thousands of poems of which only hundreds survive. The book, *The Gift*, translated by Daniel Ladinsky, is a wonderful trip through the mind of a mystic and a true spiritual journey in itself. If ever a book of spiritual poems could fill anyone reading it with laughter and love, this is it. This book could be given as a forever gift to anyone, for any purpose, at any time. The purpose of my book is to highlight some "keys" dropped by sages who have guided me in life.

# TABLE OF CONTENTS

# INTRODUCTION

*"There are two ways to look at life. One is as though nothing is a miracle; the other is as though everything is a miracle."*
**—Albert Einstein**

Life can be hard for many people. I'm guessing you already know that.

The fact is, the color of the lens through which you look at life directly affects your experience of it. This book is about how I changed the color of my lens—and you can, too.

One of the proudest insignia a man can wear in the U.S. Military is the Navy SEAL Trident. I had the privilege of serving as a U.S. Navy SEAL for 25 years and, perhaps not surprisingly, the trauma that I both witnessed and personally experienced has had a pronounced and lingering effect on me as a human being. But in my case, it is also true to say that trauma led me to reach a good place I may not have gotten to without it.

Here's the interesting thing I discovered while dealing with that: In one way or another, the vast majority of humans are impacted by trauma, leading to Post-Traumatic Stress Disorder (PTSD) or its milder residual effects. Yes, virtually all of us.

While my trauma was the legacy of combat experiences, you might give yours a different label—the death of a loved one, a messy divorce, a cancer diagnosis, the chaos of addiction, or the devastation of bankruptcy. But inevitably, we will all face some monumental struggles that can damage our well-being and threaten to change our view of the world.

That's how I became deeply interested in the ways people respond in the aftermath of trauma and the importance of the spiritual paths they can take toward healing.

This book closely examines that topic, using my life experiences as a backdrop. It's part memoir and, hopefully, part inspiration for you to explore the deeper meaning and purpose for your own life.

As you'll soon see, my life as a Navy SEAL is closely connected to many of the events I discuss in the pages ahead. I will provide a view of what those experiences were like for me, personally.

The life of a Navy SEAL is *not* all work and no play, and I hope my words will accurately capture both sides—from the seriousness of SEAL training and operations to the boisterous, life-filled nature of individual SEALs. Most of us began as young adults and matured to be grown men through the SEAL experience. And, because of our line of work, we were exposed to some horrific things along the way.

Whether you are a military combat veteran or an abuse victim or someone fighting a chronic illness, I hope the chapters that follow will provide value and support along your journey in recovering from trauma…whatever that looks like for you.

## The Goal

My principal aim with writing this book is to leave behind a trail of insight, focusing on the importance of active spirituality as a restorative tool for overcoming the many difficulties of life. I'll recount my experiences with trauma, describe my search for meaning, explain my route to personally discover what is called the metaphysical philosophy, and share some of the resources that made an enormous difference in my own life.

For more than 50 years, I've collected meaningful ideas and quotes to help answer the questions, "Who am I?" and "Why am I here?" The transformative wisdom I gained came from experts, "saints," spiritual teachers, and normal people who have opened their personal channels to information meant to help all of us on our human journeys.

The cumulative impact of that research? It was life changing—and I don't mean that in a melodramatic way. It literally changed my life, enabling me to move beyond my experience of trauma and its effects, and to discover my purpose in the bigger, broader, spiritual realm. This enabled me to find peace and happiness that I never thought would be possible.

I believe every one of us is hard-wired as a spiritual being. Sooner or later, we all long to know how we fit into this vast universe and question the spiritual purpose of our existence. That search—often intensified during or after a time of trauma—may lead people through traditional religious beliefs or to personal pathways more "outside the box."

When you find yourself on that road, I encourage you to keep looking for answers to those pivotal questions. And if this book can provide you with a roadmap along the way, I will consider it a success.

## The Main Idea

On the cover of this book is a depiction of a three-legged stool. At this point, you might be thinking, "Hey Tom, what's the deal with the three-legged stool?" I'm glad you asked.

Every one of us is, quite literally, supported by the three basic pillars of mind, body, and spirit. When those areas (the three "legs") are equally healthy, we have the strength and balance to handle whatever curveballs life throws at us. On the other hand, if one or more of those legs begins to deteriorate for whatever reason, the proverbial stool becomes unstable and tips over. It's basic physics.

Our best defense against life's traumas is to make sure all three of those legs—our mental, physical, and spiritual well-being—are strong and sturdy. But if we ignore one of them or get knocked down through no fault of our own, the fastest way to recover is to rebuild those areas and take deliberate action to re-establish our balance.

As I know firsthand, that's not an easy task, but it *is* a path forward. It's a direction. Sometimes when we feel surrounded by immense darkness, that's the light that can lead us from trauma to triumph.

## The Challenge

Over the past few centuries, the Western world has moved to increasingly idolize human intellect. That often overshadows the fact that each one of us possesses two major tools to evaluate everything around us: *our reason* and *our intuition*. Here's my challenge to you…

As you embark on a healing journey and a spiritual quest, don't overlook the power of that second tool. Your intuition is a valuable guide if you just pay attention to it. In fact, your own intuitive awareness of what is right for you is actually your most important teacher. Trust your intuition and let it be your final authority. Keep an open mind, and be willing to re-examine your life from a new perspective. Suspend any preconceived notions you might have about exploring your spiritual side.

I strongly encourage you to read the original literature and materials that I reference throughout the book. I'll share a number of paraphrased sections and quotes from these sources but, frankly, none of that can really do justice to the brilliant words of these extraordinary authors and spiritual teachers. While I will describe the impact these ideas had on my life, each person may have a different experience. The greatest gift you can give yourself is to read them on your own and see how they might apply to you.

To support that process, I've included an Appendix with a list of some of the major sources I mention in the book. You'll find some notes to add clarity at the close of many chapters, but the summarized guide to some of the sub-themes of the book at the end is my gift to you.

Although it wasn't always easy to recall some of the stories in this book, I'm grateful I had the opportunity to write it—and equally grateful that you are interested in reading it. I sincerely hope it will resonate with you and perhaps spark a new way of thinking that adds real value and meaning to your life.

Let's get started…

# CHAPTER 1
# MY WORLD VIEW

*"We don't see things as they are. We see them as we are."*
**—Anais Nin**

The pungent smells and strange sounds of the rural landscape in southern Vietnam initially overwhelm a person at night.

The air is alternatingly filled with both good, earthy smells and a bitter blend of rotting plants, sewer-tinged mud, and the distinct aromas of domestic and wild animals. Instead of silence, you often hear a full chorus of insects, the ominous rustling of foliage, and random startling noises that can play tricks on your mind.

Constant companions are the mosquitoes and the leeches, along with the stifling heat, which comes in two seasonal variations: "wet" and "dry."

This baffling combination of jungle and rice paddy, with all its sensory contradictions, is permanently etched in the minds of every combatant of the conflict which brought the American military to that country.

I landed in this peculiar environment as a brand-new officer with the U.S. Navy SEALs in 1968. The SEAL acronym stands for Sea, Air, and Land—the three basic options to insert commando units or individuals into a combat or target area. Created during the presidency of John F. Kennedy, SEAL teams were designed from the beginning to be the best trained and most aggressive military fighters on earth. Specific details about our operations were (and still are) considered classified.

As I began my first combat assignment in Vietnam, I was ready to fulfill the mission of the SEALS: to take the war to the enemy at night in a manner that would strike fear into anyone we targeted. This deadly intent went both ways. We saw leaflets posted everywhere, announcing a bounty of $50,000 U.S. dollars for any Navy SEAL killed or captured. They referred to us in Vietnamese as "The Devils with Green Faces." A little disconcerting, to say the least.

On the upside, we were prepared. A SEAL platoon always carried more fire power than any equivalent number of military personnel in any different unit. Our squad of seven SEALs had three machine guns, three M-16 automatic weapons, one grenade launcher, and one shotgun, as well as personal handguns and plenty of hand grenades and claymore mines.

Our job was to be the attacker, not the attacked. As the squad leader, I was in charge of making sure we stayed on the right end of that equation. Only once during my initial tour of duty in Vietnam was my SEAL squad caught by surprise in an ambush.

It was brutal.

The sound of bullets passing very close to your body can be likened to the sound of angry, high-speed bees. Of course, each person's reaction to being the target of gunfire is affected by a combination of personal temperament and training. But the immediate mind-body reaction is instinctive and classically referred to as the flight-or-fight response.

One purpose of our SEAL training was to minimize the human reflexive "flight" reaction, substituting an automatic "fight" response to help protect ourselves and our squad members. Specifically, we were trained to respond aggressively and to retain our sense of being a unit even under the direst circumstances.

As the Viet Cong initiated their ambush against us, three of the seven men in our squad were almost immediately wounded—including me. I was knocked to the ground by a bullet that laid open the back of my leg behind my knee. I quickly realized I had lost all function and feeling in the leg, from the hip down. One of my machine gunners was shot through the hand, but he was somehow able to continue firing. And our Platoon Chief Petty Officer was badly wounded in the head, subsequently losing one of his eyes.

The Chief Petty Officer is the senior enlisted (i.e., non-officer) leader of a platoon or group. The man who held this role in my squad had also been in charge of my initial SEAL training class, and he had been a major role model and mentor to me. Realizing the extent of his injury was personally devastating.

With the reality of the ambush upon us, we immediately began returning fire and called for helicopter gunship support, from our Navy "Seawolves" squadron, who were regularly positioned to immediately come our aid if needed. For protection and a better firing position, we all quickly crawled into the small pond and ditch alongside of a bamboo "hooch" (a thatched hut). We guided our temporarily blinded Chief Petty Officer with us along the way.

Now, let me try to paint this highly unpleasant picture for you.

This pond and ditch were used by the Vietnamese family occupying the hooch as an outdoor latrine. It was filled with feces and urine, as well as catfish that survived by eating the feces. Extremely thankful for the protection provided by this man-made trench, the overwhelming smell was only a minor annoyance.

Within minutes, one of our gunship helicopters appeared and began strafing the area in front of us with its machine gun fire. This allowed us to maneuver along the ditch and then move toward the jungle. Once there, we set up a perimeter of weapons fire that allowed a Medical Evacuation (MEDEVAC) helicopter to land and extract all my squad under the covering fire of the gunship.

We later learned that our weapons fire, combined with that of the helicopter, had killed three Viet Cong soldiers and wounded several others. Still, as the squad leader, I was haunted by this ambush, and I felt personally responsible for our squad being attacked. I had fallen short of the "be the attacker, not the attacked" objective, and that gnawed at me in a way that's not hard to understand for any SEAL.

How did we not see this coming? What could we have done differently?

Shortly after that incident, our intelligence sources helped to answer both of those questions. The Viet Cong had initially located us by tracking our boot prints in the mud to the ambush site.

From that operation on, my squad went barefoot on every mission in the Mekong Delta area.

## Processing Trauma

This was just one of many experiences I had as a Navy SEAL that up-ended my "three-legged stool."

Physically, I was injured, although it turned out my wound was minor. I returned to being fully operational within a few days.

Mentally, as the constant rhythm of operations continued, I could only compartmentalize for so long before the violent memories started seeping into my consciousness, despite my desire to move past them. After multiple ambushes and prisoner captures, I felt I had become a different person. The taking of human life creates a trauma in the human psyche, which may or may not be consciously understood as such at the time.

And spiritually? Even all those years of attending Catholic School couldn't prepare me for the deep questions about life that bubbled to the surface over time as a result of what I was experiencing.

These events did, however, prompt me to eventually do a great deal of reflection and analysis. It became obvious that traumatic events have the power to shatter our established values systems—our unique world views.

I define our "world views" as an intricate tapestry composed of our ideas, beliefs, and emotions. They are a product of our hereditary and cultural values, learnings, and behaviors. And they are not a fixed entity; they can and do change throughout our lives. For example, this book is a product of my "world view."

Regarding items in a personal values structure, maybe you value patriotism, "the good life," or the tenets of a particular religion. But in the aftermath of trauma, you may find yourself asking, "What now?" and grappling with a set of lingering, often perplexing symptoms that resist conventional rehabilitation.

That's certainly where I found myself.

So, what happens when our values and beliefs are shattered by trauma? For me, the way back to normalcy was to work on rebalancing the three-legged stool to restore my personal stability.

## Defining the Legs of the Stool

The concept of the three-legged stool was first discussed historically by several ancient Greek philosophers. Then it was carried down through the centuries by people interested in exploring humanity and the issues humans face from a religious, scientific, or philosophical point of view.

If you want to give this a present-day slant, you might compare the three-legged stool to the modern business concept known as Total Quality Management (TQM). In TQM, every product is a composite of its parts. To create a quality product, each component part must have the highest quality and maximum functionality, or the overall product quality suffers.

Seems obvious and simple, doesn't it?

And yet, when we apply it to ourselves as humans, there seems to be a disconnect. Many people treat their mind, body, and spirit as completely independent functions. They might never give any thought to the necessary relationship between them or consider how that synergy is required for a well-balanced result.

Trust me when I tell you that the integration among these three elements could not be more important. The proverbial stool needs all three legs, strong and sturdy, for us to survive and thrive.

## Looking at the Components

In thinking about our world view, it helps to dive a little deeper into the legs of our metaphorical stools. What exactly do I mean by mind, body, and spirit?

### *Mind*

Some people may tend to think of the "mind" and the "brain" as the same thing. They are not.

The *brain* is the physical apparatus which sits inside our skulls and is often the focus of much scientific research. But the *mind* includes the brain's non-physical counterparts. This intangible entity encompasses the totality of the human psyche, which incorporates our sense of consciousness, intuition, and thought processes. As I use the term, it goes beyond what science can explain and includes such things as clairvoyance, telepathy, and out-of-body experiences, which I will discuss.

Meredith Young-Sowers, the executive director of a global spiritual community and school in New Hampshire, captures some nuances involved in defining some of the functions of the mind.

> *"Conscious mind is the body's creative computer. It perceives, judges, and reflects all that is thought and experienced. These perceptions form an ever-changing complex of information. This network becomes the 'program' with which the body functions. In its capacity as filter, the conscious mind sifts through all contradictory or seemingly inappropriate incoming data, enabling it to function in what the conscious mind considers an appropriate fashion. Undesirable, contradictory, or threatening input is effortlessly filtered out of conscious reach into the super-conscious mind for storage."*[1]

The main point is that mental health is vitally important for us to function well. If our minds are the programs for our bodies, as Young-Sowers suggests, a deficit here impacts everything. It would be like trying to run a computer with a deficient operating system or bug-filled software. So, when we are recovering from trauma, the mind is a key support system and a critical component in the journey toward healing.

### *Body*

This definition is a bit more intuitive. When I refer to our bodies, I'm generally talking about the overall physical structure of a human being. I also like to think about the body as our "soul in flesh." It's a valuable and necessary vessel for us while we are alive, just like we would need space suits if we were traveling in outer space.

Since our bodies are indispensable tools, it makes good sense to treat them with care and respect. Admittedly, that involves some self-discipline and hard work. But volumes and volumes of literature have been written on the benefits of maintaining optimal fitness, much of it scientifically proven. Keeping our bodies healthy is a vital part of being strong enough to handle adversity as the second leg of our stools.

There's also plenty of scientific research today that confirms the causative link between the mind and the body. If we experience mental trauma like severe stress, we often feel the effects in our bodies. Think inflammation, chronic fatigue, heart disease, and even Alzheimer's.

The opposite is true, as well. People who are intentional about having a positive mental outlook experience regular feelings of belonging, satisfaction, and joy. Compared with people who are normally pessimistic about themselves and their lives, the positive thinkers have fewer medical issues of all types and actually tend to live longer.

Another facet of that connection? People who treat physical issues through mental tools like meditation can statistically reduce their painful symptoms.

As we look at the pathways to healing after any kind of trauma, improving our physical fitness and taking care of our bodies are essential requirements to achieve success.

### *Spirit*

This leg of the stool—the spirit—is the main focus of my book. When I refer to spirit or spirituality, I'm talking about moving toward a place in which we know that life has meaning, plus also understanding the role we play in it.

To be clear, I'm not referring to any particular religious tradition or practice, although those could certainly be part of your path if they lead you forward in a positive way to discover your own truth. With that said, many people searching for their own individual spirituality may find themselves needing to step outside of normal religious dogma. The ideas I share in this book could add value for either group.

Thomas Merton—a Trappist monk, mystic, and noted theological writer—believed that a true spiritual search doesn't go from answer to answer, as we would like. Instead, it goes from question to question. That makes the process far more difficult, but much more meaningful.[2] At least, this has been my experience.

No doubt about it, the third leg of the stool is much harder to define and quantify. But the act of seeking (and continuing to seek) a personally viable, spiritual path should be understood as the most important element in supporting the structure of our lives.

## Summing It Up

This discussion leads to some important questions.

- How would you define your world view? What ideas, emotions, and beliefs form the lens through which you see the world around you?
- How strong are the legs of your stool—your mental, physical, and spiritual health?
- What experiences in your life have damaged the legs of your stool?
- If the legs of your stool aren't optimal today, do you have a plan to change that?

Many times, answering these questions involves looking back at your past and evaluating the influences (conscious and subconscious) that have formed your view of the world. That's where we'll pick up the next chapter.

***<u>Notes:</u>***

1. Young-Sowers, Meredith Lady, *Agartha,* Stillpoint Publishing, 1984, pp. 87-89. I will be discussing the phenomenon of "channeling" and the work of this spiritual teacher as the book proceeds.
2. Stella, Tom, *A Faith Worth Believing: Finding New Life Beyond the Rules of Religion,* Harper Collins Publishers, New York, 2004, p. 14.

# CHAPTER 2
# GROWING UP

*"Philosophy is thinking about how to think about life."*
**—Emmanuel Kant**

As you begin to ponder your own world view, I want to give you some perspective on mine and how the three legs of my stool took shape from the very beginning.

## Family Life

I was born in Tucson, Arizona, in a place called "The Stork's Nest," which was one of the city's first maternity wards. It was 1943. I'm not sure if it's even possible to consciously remember being born, but I've always had a clear vision of the windowsill in that room and the doctor's hairy arm with a wristwatch. I was held upside down and spanked as a way of prompting me to take my first squalling breath.

The first two years of my life were spent with my mother, while my father served in the U.S. Army during World War II. Eventually we moved from Arizona to Wisconsin, where much of my mother's family lived.

My early memories are, of course, somewhat sporadic, but a few random ones do stand out.

When I was two years old, I remember seeing my father for the first time. He was still in the Army and either on leave or back from the war. I can envision being in our little apartment and feeling very protective of my mom. I had the distinct feeling that I didn't want him to get between me and my mother.

I also have a vivid memory from about a year later that involved my sister Sharon, who is eighteen months younger than me. Let's just say this one really shows my mischievous side. For some reason, I stole a bottle out of her crib. At least I had the good sense to hide while I was drinking it so I wouldn't get caught.

When I was four years old, my parents had a summer business selling hamburgers in Wisconsin. I was sitting on the counter and accidentally stuck my foot into the automatic electric meat grinder—*while it was grinding*. Thankfully, I was wearing a type of ankle-high leather shoes which saved my foot by jamming the blade of the machine. My dad, however, had to stick his hand into the machine to pull out my foot and was badly cut on four fingers. The adults sent me outside right away, so I didn't have to see the bloody mess. I remember limping a little but was, otherwise, unhurt.

Life-changing trauma barged in for my sister and me at an early age. When I was six and Sharon was four, our mother was killed in a tragic car accident. We were too young to process her death when it happened, but I recall being very frightened about also losing my father. It was a nagging fear that stayed with me throughout my childhood and into my late teenage years.

To help us get a fresh start, my father moved us back to Arizona in 1950. He shared his grief with a woman who had been my mother's best friend, and they subsequently got married. Our new stepmother—we called her Meemaw—adopted Sharon and me.

My dad was a gentle man, but his early life just kept giving him the short end of the stick. His own father simply disappeared when he was two years old and never surfaced again. The hurt from that abandonment stayed with him into old age.

He was on his own by the time he was 15. Two years later, our country was hit with the Great Depression. At that point, he dropped out of school and turned his part-time job at a car-repair garage into full-time employment. I'm pretty sure that wasn't how he envisioned his life going, and it must have taken a heavy toll on him. Honestly, my father never got over the draining effects of the Depression era.

That lasting trauma, combined with the death of my mother, pushed him to drink heavily. He was never angry or mean when drinking, but it did become a constant state for him—from the time he came home from work until he went to bed. Well, to be fair, he also kept a bottle by the bedside in case he needed a little chaser during the night.

Okay, let's just call it what it was: He became an alcoholic.

Despite the daily drinking, he always seemed to function well and became a sixth-grade school teacher—a job he kept until his retirement. Throughout those years, I still had that persistent fear of losing him. I always tried to be on good behavior, just in case.

My father was a living monument to the ancient maxim by Epictetus: "Wealth consists not of having great possessions, but of having few wants." As a teacher, he earned a very meager salary but consistently refused offers to become the principal at his school. His only concern and primary joy in life was our family.

We couldn't afford a swimming pool, so he purchased a plastic baby pool. He would lie in the cool water while listening to a baseball game on the radio and sipping a beer. He valued his summer months off work, and we would go almost daily to swim in the local river running through nearby Sabino Canyon in the mornings. We camped out on weekends and went out once a week for Mexican food or pizza.

My dad and I just sat and talked a lot during these times. He would tell me about some of the events of his life, and I would talk about mine. From a child's perspective, this is now called "quality time" with your parents. Dad and Meemaw literally never went anywhere without Sharon, me, and our dog. Dad's motto was "Take Life Easy." Over the years, this morphed into my current motto, "Life Is Good."

Following retirement, my father had a series of mishaps involving over-intoxication, which led him to Alcoholics Anonymous. He then spent many years working with that organization and helping other individuals make their first steps back into sobriety.

My father had a unique talent for being able to listen without judging or offering advice, and this made him a great source of comfort to Sharon and me—as well as the people working on their own recovery. Despite his challenges, he became a legend in our family and was revered as a truly wise man.

## Mental and Physical Development

Meemaw, our new stepmother, convinced my dad that parochial school would give Sharon and me a more balanced education. So, at the start of my second-grade year, we switched to Sacred

Heart Catholic School, which offered classes through 8th grade taught by Benedictine nuns. Suffice it to say, this was somewhat of a culture shock for both of us.

The classes were rigorous, and religion was the leading focus and subject. But the highlight for me was the opportunity to play a number of different sports.

Our teams were given basic sports instruction and outfitted by a Carmelite priest named Father Gilbert Burns. He was a giant of a man who was drafted to play professional football before he felt called to become a Catholic priest. No one else in the school hierarchy had even thought about offering sports or fitness activities, but Father Gilbert arrived and made it a priority.

Had Father Gilbert not been a part of my life, I might never have known the intense joy of competitive athletics that stayed with me from that time on. To this day, I still think of him as my first, non-family, male role model.

During these years I played flag football, basketball, and fast-pitch softball.

Even though we had some initial guidance from Father Gilbert, we never had a formal coach for our sports teams at Sacred Heart. Typically, we had informal "pick-up games" that involved choosing two captains who alternately selected their teams.

Since I was frequently chosen as captain and we had no formal coach, I quickly progressed to being an informal coach for all these team sports. For our inter-school games I created the rosters, determined when we needed substitutions, and selected which players to send into the game.

Through these years, sports became more and more a part of who I was. My competitive nature flourished, and I worked hard to be the best at whatever I did. As a pitcher for our fast-pitch softball team, I was virtually unhittable through my eighth-grade year. I was also the point guard for our basketball team, and I played quarterback in football.

I loved our school colors, and I remember being so excited to wear those blue and red uniforms for whatever sport I was playing. By the way, I always used the number "3" on my jerseys. At the time, I associated that with the Holy Trinity. On formal game days against other schools, our team players were allowed to wear their uniforms to class. I recall being very proud of mine.

Eighth grade was my final year at Sacred Heart. Looking back on this period of my life, I see that the body and spirit legs of my stool were supporting me while my mind was busy maturing.

My love of sports continued in high school, when I attended a large public school with a comprehensive athletics department. You might say I literally became a "sports nut," fueling a near-obsession that grew in me through adulthood. I wanted to play every sport, and I managed to be on one team or another at almost all times for many years.

From the beginning of my passion for sports, Meemaw had one rule: If my grades fell, I couldn't play. That was all it took to keep me laser-focused on my schoolwork. I wound up excelling at both academics *and* athletics.

As an aside, this desire to be an athlete also kept me from experimenting with drugs or alcohol throughout high school. I wanted to be in the best physical shape possible.

I was a hard worker, no matter what I was doing, and that allowed me to consistently achieve success. Thanks to that level of commitment, the mental and physical legs of my stool were off to a great start.

## Spiritual Growth

I began life as a Christian. I was baptized at birth and raised as a Lutheran until my mother died. In many ways, her death sparked the beginning of my own conscious, spiritual journey. Why is my mother gone? Why am I still here?

Once my stepmother was in the picture, she raised us as Roman Catholics. Religion was a centerpiece of Meemaw's life, and she knew that enrolling us at Sacred Heart Catholic School would make prayer and religious observance a regular part of everything we did.

I was eight years old on the day of my first communion, and I was fully anticipating a major life change when I first took the "host" into my mouth. My teachers had told me this little white wafer symbolized the body of Christ.

I remember being disappointed when I didn't feel something transcendent afterwards. Still, I wasn't worried. Life seemed to have meaning, and it was feeling natural to be given rules to follow—you know, those commandments.

I had to work hard to identify my many sins while still in elementary school, but I remember feeling a great sense of relief after going to confession and sharing those "transgressions" with the local priests. I went regularly. But I'll admit, I did try to avoid confessing to Father Gilbert. I certainly didn't want him to recognize my voice.

Although I didn't realize it in specific terms at the time, my primary education in a Catholic school with its underlying values structure provided a solid spiritual base for my upbringing. From an early age, my thoughts about God, church, and religion affected my behavior. The idea of a God watching over me was appealing, and I wanted to be seen by him as a "good boy."

During my years at Sacred Heart, I served as a very devout altar boy. In fact, I eventually rose to the rank of "Knight Commander" of the "Knights of the Altar." Who knew you could get a religious promotion? I was finally beginning to feel settled after some rough early years. I believed that prayer was all I needed and, of course, that God favored us Catholics.

When I was 13, I was invited as a guest to meet with a Christian youth group of some denomination to discuss Catholicism with them. As we talked, I remember being amazed at how little they seemed to know about their own religion. They had more questions than answers. What I didn't realize at the time was that they were the ones actually being open-minded. I was simply quoting from our Catholic catechism book without allowing my mind to roam beyond those well-worn pages.

That may have been a turning point for me. Add in the hormones of puberty, and I started to feel like it was almost impossible to not run afoul of all those rules. Tom Stella, an ex-Catholic priest and author, summed up the situation accurately.

> *"The burden of religion was the awful realization that, try as I might, I could not stay on the right path...that flunking religion was always a distinct possibility."*[1]

I believe many Catholic teenagers probably felt the same way, given that the list of "mortal sins" provided to us by the church was exhaustive and difficult to avoid. Maybe I *was* in danger of flunking religion and going to "hell" for my transgressions.

By my sophomore year in high school, I'd given up on going to confession, although I occasionally attended church on Sundays. I found myself spiritually adrift, mentally isolating myself from any deep thoughts about God or religion. I remained in that state for the next several decades.

I was in my early 30s when questions of spirituality once again tugged at my heart and my brain. While many of my peers happily found great hope and faith in Christianity or one of the earth's many other religious movements—which I applaud—I felt compelled to push beyond my Catholic upbringing for answers. I was in search of a personally meaningful experience of truth, and I honestly had no idea what that would look like.

***Note:***

1. Stella, Tom, *A Faith Worth Believing*, op. cit., Harper One, 2011, p. 14.

# CHAPTER 3
# CHOOSING A PATH

*"There are two questions that we have to ask ourselves. The first is, 'Where am I going?' and the second is, 'Who will go with me?'"*
**—Howard Thurman**

In 1962, when I graduated from high school, our nation had a military draft. Anyone in my age group who was mentally and physically fit (and didn't have an exemption) was eligible to be drafted into the U.S. Armed Forces. Since my family had no funds to help me at any follow-on university, I was at risk of being drafted unless I found a way to enter college.

My dad had been in the Army, spending most of his time deployed in the South Pacific during World War II and rising to the rank of Corporal. His only advice to me on the subject was this: If I was going to go into the military, go in as an officer.

Having been a good student throughout high school and a three-sport varsity athlete, I found that, after taking all the scholastic and physical tests for entrance requirements, I had been offered appointments to all four of the military academies. Nearing high school graduation day, I chose the Navy. I had never been around the ocean, so why not?

## Getting Started

Our class at the Naval Academy began in mid-summer of 1962 with around 1,300 of us "plebes." An interesting statistic was that around 40% of our incoming class had played varsity football in high school, meaning they were also physically tough. Four years later, only 868 of us graduated. Most of the dropouts occurred in the first year because of how hard it was to be a "plebe."

Halfway through my plebe year, I had just about had enough and wasn't feeling good about my decision to be at the Academy. But as soon as I left home in Arizona the previous summer, my parents started a house remodel which expanded their bedroom by taking over the space which my bedroom had occupied. When I finally received permission to return home for Christmas, the only place left for me to sleep in our house was the couch in the living room.

Any thoughts I had about not returning to the Naval Academy evaporated with this understanding. I have often wondered how many of those who quit that first year knew they had a bedroom to which they could return.

The building which houses the midshipmen at the Academy is named Bancroft Hall and was commonly referred to as "Mother Bancroft." It did become home to me while I was there. There truly is something positive to say about the net result of the complete immersion that a midshipman or cadet goes through during this process.

The methods utilized to teach rules about discipline and responsibility at the Academy were extremely harsh, and they have since been modified with the inclusion of women as midshipmen. Some of the hazing was quite literally brutal by today's standards, but there was, at the core of it, a learned discipline that has served me and others well as we have gone on with our lives in the Navy and beyond.

I was secretly a rebel plebe, and I hated the hazing. I wasn't deeply interested in the Navy lore or the courses relating to the parts of the Navy I was being exposed to. Nonetheless, I settled into life at the Naval Academy by my second year, and I never again thought seriously about not graduating.

The normal routine at the Academy was 5-½ days of classes weekly, with free time on Saturday afternoons and Sundays after your choice of religious service. I was a good student and never had any concerns about course grades.

From a roommate, I learned something that served me well: "Keep your mouth shut and your shoes shined." Applying this dictum meant that we kept our opinions to ourselves, which allowed us to do pretty much as we pleased during our free times. It became clear that my roommate and I were both looking avidly for a better future for ourselves.

While at the Naval Academy, I played varsity football on the 150-pound team. I also boxed, winning the Brigade welterweight boxing championship in my last year there. These competitive sports, plus the Academy's mandatory and rigorous intramural sports programs, kept me physically active all year, every year. In addition, the school's extremely advanced regimen kept me in an overall optimistic and largely happy mood, despite my general dislike for hierarchy and what little I knew about life in the main branches of the Navy.

## Rethinking my Spirituality

Sunday religious service attendance was mandatory at the Academy, so I went to Catholic Mass each week for all four years I was there. Well, truthfully, I looked for reasons to avoid it whenever I could. But when I arrived, the first order of business was finding a comfortable spot so I could "snooze" without being seen by the watchful "Officer of the Day." If you got caught? The offense was punishable by four hours of marching with your rifle around the Academy square. I honestly don't remember much about the church services—except for trying not to doze off.

I was very familiar with the Bible, the sacraments, and the commandments of the Catholic Church, but I didn't feel personally affected by my attendance in the ceremonies. At the time, skipping church was considered a mortal sin by the Catholic Church and punishable by eternal damnation in hell. That was quite a psychological load to carry around for a young man, and I resolved it by giving up on prayer and becoming an agnostic.

Following church on Sundays, we would go back through the still-darkened halls to the dining room, where I would have eggs and pancakes. Then I would go back to my room and sleep until the Sunday noon formation.

During this period, I was becoming aware of the social aspects of religion as it affected various parts of the world. In particular, I thought about South America, where there was a movement toward trying to actually help the poor and hungry by priests outside confines of the church doctrines, but in a practical way. This was causing social unrest for the governments and the Catholic Church in those parts of the world, and many priests found themselves treated as revolutionaries.

It was disconcerting to me that the Catholic Church and many of its subsequent Christian offshoots have always had a moral precept to help the poor and oppressed, while at the same time most often aligning with the ruling, wealthy, and military groups in each country. Intentional or not, this connection seemed to justify the internal "cleansings" and the bloody wars, along with the killing of innocent people that always accompany these actions. I became disenchanted by how religion has been used by one side or the other to justify or support so many wars and killing throughout history.

This is not to blame or disparage the many dedicated priests, monks, nuns, and religious organizations and personages who have been and are genuinely committed to peace on earth and to the poor and down-trodden people throughout the globe. Instead, a broader view of religious organizations through a historical lens presents a tendency that does not sit well in review.

I found myself with a feeling that attendance at church by itself was not satisfying me, on top of the social misgivings I was having about the Roman Catholic Church in particular.

I believe that it was a famous English mystic who said that attending church for many is like reading a menu and listening to a discussion about food, but without ever actually having a meal and tasting real food. This describes the overall experience for me.

## Finding a Purpose

Despite that disconnect, I still sensed the importance of believing that life has meaning and figuring out what role we play as part of our purpose. That instinct was correct—for people of all ages.

When children don't have any grounding beliefs, they see no reason to pay attention and be engaged in school. We tend to blame the teachers, the curriculum, or the school board for their disinterest. The truth is, students who have a sense of purpose and want to learn have historically done so, and continue to do so, often under truly adverse conditions.

Scientific research now posits that children tend to succeed when they believe that life has meaning. In her book, *The Spiritual Child*, Dr. Lisa Miller, Ph.D., a clinical psychologist and director of the clinical psychology program at Teachers College, Columbia University, states that we have overwhelming medical evidence through clinical studies that children are "hardwired" to be interested in spirituality and the meaning of things.

Particularly during the second decade of life, children begin their search to understand themselves and their lives. This can be referred to as the "Hero's Journey" as named by Joseph Campbell, or simply as a spiritual search, as referenced by many authors.[1]

Not surprisingly, if children are encouraged by their families and cultures to seek understanding and meaning in their lives, they can flourish and grow in a holistic way, leading them to confront their challenges more positively and with better outcomes. In other words, they have strength and balance among the three legs of the stool we all stand on.

For another example, I later worked with a task force appointed by the Chief of Naval Operations. Our charge was to examine why many of the Navy's remedial programs (e.g., to lose weight, stop smoking, give up alcohol, etc.) were not getting good results. The conclusion of the task force was that the "spirit leg" of the metaphorical stool was weak or missing among the sailors struggling with these issues. This ultimately led to the creation of the Navy's Personal Excellence Program, which used a more holistic approach to support these individuals.

The lesson is basically the same for adults *and* children. Believing that your life has purpose is a significant predictor of success in whatever you attempt to do.

## Looking Ahead

During my senior year, I began to be concerned about my future. I had chosen the Naval Academy largely because it was a fully-paid-for education, and I wanted to play football there. I hadn't really thought about the follow-on responsibilities of being in the Navy.

In retrospect, I believe the personal benefits of spending some time "in service" are being largely overlooked. Also of note, for every serviceman or woman who wants to carry a gun or engage in actual combat operations, there are twelve individuals in support capacities that don't require any active combat.

There's also a great opportunity for individuals to join the military and have the service pay for them to become doctors, dentists, lawyers, computer experts, or you-name-it in so many other professional fields. Not only can a person wind up as what they want to be without any debt, the military service pays the person in these programs a full salary while a student.

None of this was actively mentioned to me, nor did it occur to me while I was a midshipman at the Naval Academy. I had a very short-sighted view of military opportunities.

Despite the recent great increase in public accolades for men and women in our armed services ("thank you for your service"), the norm for the sons and daughters of most Americans is to avoid situations resembling military discipline, service, and routines as much as possible. Today, less than one half of 1% of our population is in the Armed Forces.

In my mind, this has led to something resembling a gladiator experience. Very few individuals are serving, fewer yet are actually fighting. And most citizens are willing to embrace and take for granted their life's comforts while not involved at all.

The Navy clearly forced me to grow up and assess myself as an individual at an early age. I can see that there was an overall good in this discipline and milieu which I simply would not have had at that age if left to my own devices.

## Preparing to Graduate

After three years at the Naval Academy, I spent my final summer before the fourth year there as an exchange midshipman assigned to the Venezuelan Navy. It was both an intense and a thoroughly enjoyable summer. I was accompanied by another midshipman, Mike Wunsch, from the Naval Academy, and we became fast friends. Mike was a light-heavyweight wrestler and was nicknamed "Meat Nose" by our academy classmates.

At that time, a book called *Beat the Dealer* was published. It claimed that the gambling game of blackjack could be beaten by giving each card in the card deck a value, and then placing bets depending on the status of the remainder of the card deck. Mike and I became fascinated by this book and visited various casinos during the summer. We vowed we would learn how to count cards and "beat the dealers."

Upon our return to the Naval Academy at summer's end, Mike and I recruited two other midshipman and formed a "gang" dedicated to learning how to count cards. After buying two other newly published books with card-counting systems, our goal was to get permission to use the Academy computer lab from midnight to 6 a.m. to calculate a comparison between the systems and select the best one.

At that time, computers were truly in their infancy. Our first job was to translate these card-counting systems into the rudimentary computer language called FORTRAN and then play many hours of comparison on the computer. Looking back on this, we should have gotten some academic credit for our efforts, if not for the desired end use of our work.

We selected the best system and began the hard work of learning to count values for every card dealt out—all while pretending to not be concentrating as hard as we were. We developed "flash cards" to review each potential card combination we could be dealt, based on our overall deck calculations.

We commandeered the building cleaner's equipment closet, again at night, for our rehearsals. We put a blanket up around the inside of the door to shut out any light, and we played blackjack in near silence so as not to be discovered by the Officer of the Watch. We practiced and practiced. We deserved an "A" for effort.

Upon graduation, we all had two months of free time (called "leave" in the Navy) before reporting for duty as officers. That was our chance to try out our card-playing skills, so we embarked on our big adventure.

We visited casinos in the Bahamas, Panama, Reno, and Las Vegas, and we played blackjack every day for hours on end. We kept a meticulous record of each day's activity, and we pooled all our earnings each night. Let's just say we had a thoroughly good time using our winnings—staying in nice hotels and flying on commercial airlines between locations.

Only one of us was caught card-counting by a casino manager during the entire trip. The bouncer who escorted my friend to the door said to him, "Mister, this is a credit to your card-playing ability, but we don't want you playing here anymore." He took that as a compliment.

At the end of our leave period, we split up the remaining funds in our "kitty" and each went our separate ways. Three of us would stay in the Navy, while Mike Wunsch joined the Marine Corps.

Although the war in Vietnam was growing in intensity at that time, I can't remember us discussing it at all. What we didn't know was that, within two years, two of the four of us—my classmates Mike Wunsch (Marine) and Pat Buckley (Navy pilot)—would be dead because of that war.

***Note:***

1. Campbell, Joseph, *The Hero's Journey*, New World Library, 2014.

# CHAPTER 4
# JUMPING OFF THE PIER

*"A ship in a harbor is safe. But that is not what ships are built for."*
**—John Shedd**

I graduated from the Naval Academy in 1966 as an Ensign in the United States Navy. My first assignment was that of a student officer at the Naval Flight School in Pensacola, Florida. However, I rapidly discovered that Naval aviation was *not* what I wanted to do. My year in Pensacola was one of the few times in my life in which I felt that I had made a bad choice, given the options available to me.

I continued to submit transfer request "chits" to enter the Underwater Demolition Team/SEAL Team (UDT/SEAL) training school. At that time, I was a strong student in good standing in the Naval Flight Officer (NFO) class. But we were also involved as a nation with what was quickly becoming the Vietnam War, so the Navy was looking for candidates for UDT/SEAL work as a priority. As a result of this, I was offered the opportunity to transfer into the UDT/SEAL training program (officially called Basic Underwater Demolition and SEAL Training or BUD/S). That set my life's overall professional course for the next 25 years.

It is hard to overstate the joy I felt upon entering UDT/ SEAL training. The pure physicality of it was exactly what I needed. My goal at the time was simply to get through training and then deploy to the Mediterranean with a UDT detachment aboard an amphibious ship. My vision of this lifestyle was lots of swimming, beach volleyball, and "liberty" calls in interesting ports.

I had given no thought of any depth to the work or lifestyle of an actual Navy SEAL, and I hadn't heard anything about it prior to the training. The SEAL program was classified, meaning confidential to outsiders. In fact, when we first arrived for our assignment, many of the wives literally had no idea what their husbands did in the Navy.

What I did know was that the training would be intense.

I was very lucky in getting into a class that started in Little Creek, Virginia, in April. I finished up several months later after spending time in Key West, Florida, and Roosevelt Roads, Puerto Rico. This meant that I spent most of my training time in warm weather and warm-water environments.

Regardless of the temperatures, statistics say that approximately 80% of every UDT/SEAL training class will voluntarily quit or drop out "involuntarily" prior to graduation. Thinking about this just a little bit should tell anyone interested in becoming a SEAL that it pays to stay in the top 20% of each graded training event.

Life in the bottom half of a SEAL training group was made pure hell by the instructors. The top half weren't getting it any easier in terms of effort. But as long as a trainee was excelling among his peers, he had a much better chance of getting through.

## Surviving "Hell Week"

Much has been written about the rigors of UDT/SEAL training. In particular, publicity often surrounds what they call "Hell Week." It's a fact that nobody is happy during Hell Week, so I will discuss it briefly without dwelling on it.

Hell Week occurs after an initial five-week period of vigorous training. It's five and one-half days of virtually nonstop movement and exercise with little or no sleep. Total sleep hours during the week do not exceed four hours.

All during Hell Week, trainees wear light helmets and collectively carry rubber boats on their heads pretty much everywhere they go. Running is mandatory, even with the boat hammering down on their heads. Many of the training events and challenges require teamwork and cooperation, and teams win or lose, not the individual.

The boats with paddles weigh between 200 and 300 pounds. A normal boat crew starts with eight trainees under the boat. If a trainee simply can't go on and wants to resign, all he has to do is take off his helmet and stop. He will be finished immediately and will return to the UDT/SEAL compound to "ring the bell" as a formal sign of quitting.

As people drop out, the remaining trainees in the boat crew have to carry around more and more of the boat's weight. Once a crew is reduced to four trainees, they are placed into the reduced ranks of another boat crew and proceed as before.

One purpose of Hell Week is to demonstrate that the body can and will continue to perform well past the point where the mind says it can't go on any further. A secondary purpose of this week is to drive home, in the most physical and mental ways possible, the importance of your team as the functional unit. There is simply no way to get through this week without teamwork, and this is repeatedly demonstrated.

## Pushing the Limits

Halfway through Hell Week, we had gone three days almost nonstop with no sleep. As the sun came up, we ran with our boats to breakfast. We were allowed to walk back to the barracks after eating—still with the boats on our heads, of course.

We were given a thirty-minute break. With no special announcement, we set out on a run. All through UDT/SEAL training we wore boots, not tennis shoes or running shoes. Though nothing had been said to us about how far we were going, our first seven miles of the run was in soft sand. We then stopped for a quick water break.

We continued to run for an additional twenty miles on the roads and trails around the Amphibious Base at Little Creek, Virginia. We then put our boats back on our heads and ran to lunch. After an hour of free time, we loaded our boats on our heads and ran down to the beach, where we went on a twelve-mile paddle. Afterward was the obstacle course, followed by mud-crawl work and log physical training (meaning each boat crew had one massive tree log that required full team work to do the exercises with it).

Wash, rinse, repeat. That went on for three more days.

Following Hell Week, basic training continued for another three weeks before Phase Two began. Phase Two included SCUBA (Self-Contained Underwater Breathing Apparatus) and closed-circuit diving training conducted in Key West,

Florida. Then Phase Three, the last major training phase prior to graduation and being assigned to an actual UDT or SEAL team, involved long-distance swimming, land warfare, weapons training, and heavy demolition training in Puerto Rico.

Hell Week aside, I remember feeling truly happy with the physical requirements and found the nature of the experience to be quite interesting. I largely felt an overpowering sense of well-being during these latter periods. As young men in the best physical shape of our lives, we mostly reveled in the daily routines. We seemed to have plenty of extra energy for every challenge they put to us, including "jungle rules" volleyball in the off hours.

## Getting Wet

One of the training exercises that UDT/SEALS go through involves cast and recovery from a fast-moving boat out in the open ocean. This essentially means dropping over the side of the motor launch at high speed into a rubber boat tied to its side, and then rolling out of the rubber boat into the water. The speed of the boat literally drives the swimmer 10-15 feet underwater.

With the extreme heat, the smell of the boat engine fumes, and the sound of the roaring motors, the shock of being underwater and the coolness and quiet down there was wonderful.

The first time I did this exercise in Puerto Rico, I was overwhelmed with the beauty of the underwater scene. The sudden silence was a great relief. The clarity of the water was such that you could see for hundreds of feet in each direction.

It was very much like being in a giant fishbowl, since we could see manta rays, sharks, turtles, and other undersea creatures moving around naturally while we were doing our thing on the surface. I stayed under water that first time as long as I could. My first impression of that still lingers with me to this day.

During our final training exercise, we swam from the island of Vieques off the coast of Puerto Rico back to the Naval Station at Roosevelt Roads. It involved approximately nine swimming miles if we caught the current and tides favorably.

Over the course of the day, our group broke into two subgroups. My swim partner and I remained with the first group, landing in Puerto Rico after approximately 10 hours of swimming. The second group missed the tide, and it took them almost 13 hours to finally enter the bay and arrive at Roosevelt Roads. That demonstrates why an ongoing SEAL motto during training is, "It pays to be a winner."

What I remember about that swim was the sharks that followed us for a large part of it, simply interested in what we were doing. I also recall the feeling of tiredness (but not exhaustion) that I had as I climbed out of the water.

No allowance was made the next day for having done anything difficult the previous day. We still began with a long, early morning run and went through a normal day of training. Another motto that summed up the experience was, "The only easy day was yesterday."[1]

Although much of the final phases of UDT/SEAL training focused on warfare techniques and skills required, I did not give much serious consideration to the probable outcome of all this preparation.

## Continuing the Training

Upon graduation from our basic training, I was initially assigned to UDT-22 in Little Creek, Virginia. That fed my vision of myself as a "frogman" with a UDT platoon assigned to a Navy amphibious ship in the Mediterranean, cruising from port to port, with free time in each port.

Teaming up with six other officer graduates from my BUD/S class, we immediately rented a seven-bedroom mansion directly on the water in Virginia Beach, and we established what was referred to in Navy terms as a "snake ranch" (meaning you couldn't trust any of your buddies alone with your date). Our minds were on things other than war.

My first assignment upon arriving at UDT-22 was to attend and graduate from the U.S. Army's airborne parachuting training at Fort Benning, Georgia. From a physical standpoint, this was fairly easy after UDT/SEAL training, and we mostly had a good time during the three weeks there.

Immediately upon my return to Norfolk, I received orders transferring me to SEAL Team Two, which was also in Virginia Beach, Virginia. The prospect of actually going into military combat then became a virtual certainty, and I received the news with a feeling that I had been cheated out of my Mediterranean cruise. At the same time, I was also filled with excitement about going into combat as a Navy SEAL.

Two months later, I was ordered to attend the U.S. Army's Ranger training in the middle of a very bad winter. The Army's method of inducing combat fatigue was long forced marches, reduced meals, and strenuous, multi-day training exercises where you slept, when you could, sitting up against a buddy in the snow. (No sleeping bags, fires, or other conveniences were allowed.)

As an aside, we began that Ranger class with 4 SEALS and approximately 100 Army types. The only way to get out of this training was to be declared medically unfit by a doctor. Trench foot, pneumonia, and frost bite were common causes for dropouts. All 4 SEALs graduated and received the Ranger patch, along with around 15 Army individuals. I realized how lucky I had been that my initial UDT/SEAL training had occurred in mostly warm weather with warm water.

One of the SEALs in my Ranger class was my friend and co-house-owner John “Bubba” Brewton. One of the techniques everyone had to learn was how to build a rope bridge across a river that would allow us to bring over men and equipment. Bridge construction starts by having someone swim one rope across the river and tie it to a tree on the other side.

Considering that it was a brutally cold winter (and not every Army guy in the class was a good swimmer!), the instructors would always call out, “Are there any SEALs in this group?” Bubba and I were usually huddled up in the back trying to look inconspicuous.

The next thing we knew, we were the volunteers who had to strip naked and swim the icy river with the rope. That was the easy part. Once on the other side, still naked, we had between 45 minutes and an hour to wait before the bridge could be completed and our clothes ferried over. We just started running in place, facing each other, to keep motivated and to keep from freezing solid.

One related incident has stuck in my memory. We were on about the tenth day of a long patrol, not having eaten much, slept much, nor shaved. I remember looking at Bubba as we were running in place and shouting, “God, I hope I don’t look as bad as you do.” We laughed about it later.

By the time I finished all of the SEAL training courses—Army Ranger School, the Survival, Escape and Evasion school, “kitchen-demolition” school, combat medicine training, jungle warfare school, Vietnamese language school, and SEAL platoon pre-deployment training before deployment to Vietnam—I was feeling about as fully trained and ready for whatever was coming next as any man could be.

## Going Undercover

Someone in the higher ranks decided that SEALs should know more about an unnamed agency, and so several of us were sent to a covert basic training program. Along with tradecraft like dead-drops and coding techniques, we were assigned practical experience in following persons of interest in a big-city environment.

One day I found myself teamed up with a SEAL Senior Chief, trailing a suspect on the streets of a major U.S. city. It was a hot summer day. We were trying not to lose our target without being spotted—all while being graded on our technique.

The Senior Chief had a rock jaw, barrel chest, and biceps bigger than my thighs. Besides not being able to keep him focused on the target rather than passing ladies, I could tell that we weren't exactly blending into the background. It would have been hard to ***not*** notice us, given his size and demeanor. We were fish out of water in that world. It was truly a comical experience, but interesting looking back on it.

## Enjoying the Ride

Between training schools and the daily training routine at Seal Team Two, my world seemed full of interesting things and experiences. Although there was a war taking place with SEAL platoons fighting in Vietnam, life in Little Creek between deployments was riotous and entertaining.

I remember being invited to the first party at the home of my Commanding Officer of SEAL Team Two. I was drinking my first beer when a whole group of SEALs came by, carrying a fellow SEAL stripped buck-naked. They hauled him through the crowd of men and women on his way to get a dunk in the ocean for his birthday. He turned out later to be my direct boss and a lifelong friend.

Shortly after that, my Commanding Officer began wrestling with the Commanding Officer of UDT-22, who was busy grilling hamburgers. Somehow in the scuffle, he wound up getting tossed on top of his grill.

Another memory from that day? My Commanding Officer's wife wore a T-shirt that said, "So many men. So little time."

I realized I had found my people.

## Valuing Physical Strength

Looking back on the entire early period of my life, I am struck by how intense physical exercise always counterbalanced any deep feelings of upset or insecurity about the future. I wonder why more emphasis is not given to this by health professionals trying to help individuals with mental health issues—especially people trying to raise normal children and teenagers. People in good physical shape are, by and large in my experience, happier and more energetic than their counterparts in accomplishing their goals, whatever those are.

Research now proves that exercise physiologically releases chemicals in the brain that contribute to a sense of health and well-being, which also encourages learning. This ties directly back to the ancient Greek understanding of the interlocking importance of mind, body, and spirit. The three-legged stool concept was right on target.

As for the three-legged stool I was standing on at this time, I would say that the mind and body legs felt strong and supportive.

The spiritual leg of my stool was asleep.

***<u>Note:</u>***

1. For an excellent book more fully outlining the rigors of basic UDT/SEAL training and "Hell Week" (and of the life of a combat Navy SEAL specifically) I recommend *SEAL Warrior* by Thomas H. Keith and J. Terry Riebling, St. Martin's Press, 2009.

# CHAPTER 5
# BOOTS ON THE GROUND

*"The downside is that war is an ugly business to be good at."*
**—Adam Makos/*Spearhead***

I arrived in Saigon, Vietnam, in May 1968, with a platoon of Navy SEALs. For reference, a SEAL platoon normally consisted of two "squads" of seven individuals. This was three months after the beginning of the famous Tet offensive in South Vietnam by North Vietnam.

As we approached landing, the pilot informed us that the airport was under attack, so we quickly unpacked our weapons and ammunition. We prepared to leave the plane upon touchdown as a fighting force. There was a certain amount of chaos on the ground, but the mortar attack was largely over as we landed. We moved quickly across the city to our lodging site.

Three days later, we were on our first operation in the Mekong Delta area around the small city of MyTho. It was customary in that era for an officer from the SEAL platoon being relieved to help plan and guide the initial operations of the incoming platoon. On our first three or four missions, we had that help. After that, I was on my own as leader whenever my squad acted independently—which was almost every other night for the next six months.

In our area of operations, large enemy forces were constantly moving about, and the surrounding countryside was heavily booby trapped. Extreme caution was required both during and after insertion for any operation, and the actual chance of enemy contact was high all the way through extraction of our platoon back to our base camp area.

## Combat Deployment

To give an example of a typical SEAL combat deployment, I went out on around 60 direct-action missions during my first tour. A direct-action mission is one whose normal purpose is to kidnap, ambush, or blow up something or someone. We made enemy contact of some type on about half of these operations. This contact often resulted in a firefight or straight capture (called a "body snatch") of a specific Viet Cong or North Vietnamese Army person-of-interest. In other cases, we conducted a trail or canal ambush for any enemy personnel moving into our "kill zone."

Many of our missions resulted in our taking prisoners. Since we were on the ground among non-combatants before and after each action, it soon became apparent that there was very little difference between the Vietnamese on our side ("the good guys") and the Vietnamese on the other side ("the bad guys"). In fact, we started to recognize that the "bad guys" were often just teenagers living in a very difficult environment, while the "good guys" were living in barracks, eating well, and often reluctant to fight. All of this has been well documented.

Other SEAL missions include hostage, downed pilot, or prisoners-of-war rescue; recapture of U.S. or allied assets occupied by opposing forces, such as captured ships or oil rigs; reconnaissance missions; and training of other foreign special operations forces. Additionally, SEALs now perform all the missions previously handled by Underwater Demolition Teams, such as beach reconnaissance for amphibious troop landing sites and underwater obstacle demolition.

Needless to say, a great spirit of team cohesion developed among all SEAL platoons. Everyone's life and safety depended on the other members of the platoon.

## Mixed Emotions

It is difficult to describe the emotions I felt as a young SEAL officer in Vietnam. I look back now at some of the things we did with sincere remorse. But the overwhelming feeling at the time (by those not wounded) was an adrenaline rush, excitement mixed with fatigue, and a hint of apprehension because of the danger. But we were always looking forward to the next operation.

This adrenaline "high" was psychologically addicting, and anyone who didn't feel it didn't thrive as a SEAL. I recall only one or two individuals out of all who served with me who clearly should not have been SEALs. After my 25 years of service, I can confidently say that most SEALs were extremely proud of their skills and their line of work, were deeply committed to their teammates as a group, and were outwardly happy with their general lifestyle.

## The Morality Question

Like most combat veterans, I went off to war thinking that it was my duty to defend the nation. At the time, I didn't believe that killing in a combat zone had any semblance to the crime of murder. We didn't have any time to really contemplate that either. During my years as a SEAL, religious services were never part of a deployed platoon's normal activities. Any personal religious beliefs were generally kept private by anyone holding them.

As the years passed and I saw our country involved in combat all around the globe, thoughts about the moral legitimacy of our actions began to grow in my mind. These thoughts were compounded by further information about the number of truly innocent people killed or maimed in each place and war zone.

The morality of killing in war is a philosophical question that is as old as warfare itself.

From the beginning of time, nations have sent their young men and women to defend their countries with an unquestioned license to kill, on the basic premise that killing in war is lawful. This notion is confirmed in mainstream literature which commonly projects death in war as simply a matter of course.

Although governments sanction killing the enemy as legitimate and morally acceptable, scientific studies conclude that killing in war leaves many combat veterans with long-lasting psychological scars. It is worth pondering that a devout adherence to differing sets of tribal, national and/or religious principles has resulted in humans killing humans in situation after situation on earth, with both sides feeling morally justified while doing it.

The general issue about violence and the taking of life is a complex one. It has been said that, at times, war is a necessary evil. I do believe there is a moral justification and imperative to stop aggression against yourself or other innocent people. I also think it's a big step from that departure point to justify all killing in all military conflicts as moral. In my opinion, there is a significant difference between the reasons for, and methods involved in, the taking of human lives.

Most people agree that war is sometimes necessary to end evil, and I believe that certain situations justify the use of force to stop atrocities. But humans should think hard before deciding that killing is appropriate as a punishment, or for retribution, or as a means to settle political differences between countries. Murder in support of a country or an ideal is still murder.

Lastly, killing in the name of God would be abhorrent to any loving deity, and it is not justified by most of the world's major religious belief systems in their original intent and form.

## The Paradox of Combat

I am writing this from my perspective now, not from the perspective of myself as a younger man. But during my time as an active SEAL, my overall attitude could best be summed up by the motto emblazoned on a T-shirt I used to wear, which said: "Peace Through Fire Superiority."

To be honest, everything about SEAL work was interesting to me—from planning the operations, to coordinating logistics for actual team insertion and extraction, to the strategy for movements once arriving at a target site, to the actions of combat as the engagement erupted. My training was thorough, and I was prepared.

Reflecting on it now, I see that SEAL activities can be viewed as amoral by their very nature. Designed as an organization to take "direct action" against persons or things, it's hard to characterize some of these activities as moral when looked at objectively. Although they are authorized by the U.S. Government and ordered by the military chain of command, SEAL operations on the ground or at sea often involve decisions that are not pre-planned. The unexpected is the norm during the course of an ambush or firefight. In a matter of moments, a SEAL squad could go from being "the hunters" to being "the hunted."

I have come to realize that the line between good and evil doesn't run between individuals, separating them into groups of "the good" and "the evil." Instead, it runs *through* each individual.

It is a time-tested procedure to take a young, normally well-adjusted civilian and, under the cloak of patriotism or religious imperative, get him or her to begin taking lives. There have always been some individuals strong enough to resist the pressures of culture, church, or country who decide not to participate in the taking of lives for any reason. There were none of these people among my associates.

The reality of the frontline combat soldier often presents this dilemma in very dramatic and personal terms. Individuals react in different ways when finding themselves in situations where the taking of human lives is unavoidable.

The issue is complicated by the differences between what is seen as necessary killing in combat, and murder. This topic is further blurred by the fact that the actual participants in many armed conflicts have necessarily opted to give the responsibility for determining the appropriateness of an actual combat situation to others rather than themselves.

Certainly, this was the case for most operations labeled as "unconventional warfare" or "special operations." These are situations in which officials who aren't personally on site decide about the necessity of action or the morality of special operations forces even being in a given country at all.

Many combat activities, and most SEAL operations, are conducted in an environment in which it is not always possible to ensure the safety of non-combatants in the vicinity of the direct action. In the case of SEAL operations in hostile environments, immediate decisions must be made concerning all casualties. In these situations, humane considerations concerning the wound severity of the enemy and involved civilians can be secondary to the overall safe extraction of both the healthy and the wounded friendly participants.

The problem is, killing in war triggers a moral crisis for many veterans who later find themselves struggling with their self-image, in their relationships with those they love most, and with their spirituality.

## The Psychological Dilemma

I specifically remember a part of our basic UDT/SEAL training that cut to the core of this mental contradiction. The instructor challenged our class with a hypothetical dilemma concerning a secret operation in a foreign country. We were told that it was of primary national importance that no one knew U.S. forces were ashore in this country and were responsible for the operation.

In this theoretical scenario, SEALS on their way to the extraction point were spotted by a woman and child. Although they were innocents, they could still obviously divulge the fact that they had seen the SEALs. Since they could not be taken prisoner and loaded back onto the submarine at sea, the dilemma was what to do with them.

The attitude the instructors were looking for was a willingness to do whatever was necessary with the woman and child—if *not* doing so would compromise the mission. I don't remember having any trouble with my understanding that we were capable of doing that, if required. What wasn't taught was the potential psychological impact of such actions, which can last a lifetime. And they often do.

## The Aftermath

The world has seen significant changes since my retirement in 1992, including shifts in every country in which SEALs operate. I transitioned to a follow-on career in business that has nothing to do with military special operations, so I certainly can't speak to the activities or mindsets of SEALS since that time.

The implicit and explicit tasks expected of Navy SEALs (or other special operations personnel) are not for everyone, and less violent careers could be chosen. With that said, I still believe that all life-path choices are valid in the bigger scheme of things. Whatever journey a human chooses will contain valuable learning experiences—ones which are probably needed by that person.

The basic SEAL attitude is that SEALs should be ready and willing to go and do whatever missions are assigned in any country. It wasn't our job to determine which side was morally right or wrong.

But when looking back since World War II, there are very few years in which U.S. forces have *not* been deployed for training foreigners and/or fighting themselves in multiple foreign places. Unfortunately, historical analysis shows that the sides we favored were often mired in greed and corruption, with little or no moral compass.

Beyond that, the toll of war usually extends well past simply those individuals engaged in the actual fighting. Consider the conflicts like our major world wars and in places like Vietnam, Afghanistan, Iraq, Ukraine and, most recently, the Gaza Strip. The traumatic impact is often monumental for people who have done nothing more than be born or live in these areas at the wrong time.

For me, the justifications and "morality" of war had become a very gray area.

# CHAPTER 6
# OUR HUMAN EXPERIENCE: PTSD

*"All laws are silent in the time of war."*
**—Thomas Hobbes**

Forty years after retiring from the U.S. Marine Corps, a former Marine (and life-long friend of mine) woke up in a cold sweat. He'd had a vivid dream of being back in the war. He could see the point man of his platoon killing a Vietnamese male farmer who accidentally startled him. Running forward in the dream, he saw the dead farmer surrounded by his wife and two small children who were wailing over their loss.

My friend was visibly shaken and could not understand the overwhelming impact of the dream. Later that day, he was sitting in his car and sobbing uncontrollably as he thought about it. Only then did my friend realize that the dream had actually been a reality—one he had "buried in a foxhole" in his mind.

## Exploring PTSD

Post-Traumatic Stress Disorder (PTSD) is an anxiety response that occurs after an individual experiences, witnesses, or participates in an event that is shocking, terrifying, or dangerous. Wide-scale interest in PTSD has grown in the United States since the beginning of the U.S. intervention in Vietnam and, subsequently, through what some have called our "perpetual wars" in Iraq and Afghanistan.

According to the National Institute of Mental Health, the symptoms of this disorder include:

- Being easily startled
- Feeling tense, on guard, or on edge
- Having difficulty concentrating
- Struggling to fall asleep or stay asleep
- Feeling irritable and having angry or aggressive outbursts
- Engaging in risky, reckless, or destructive behavior

This disorder has varying degrees of severity, and the symptoms can flare in response to some type of trigger that immediately takes the mind back to the stress-inducing event. Post-traumatic effects can include nightmares, inappropriate behavior to otherwise normal stimuli, and feelings of rage out of proportion to the triggering event. The traumatic condition can begin in a state of near panic and extreme mental or physical pain if life-changing circumstances are the result of an original disease or dysfunction cause.

It's fairly obvious how this relates to combat veterans, but I believe a majority of individuals have had or will endure some form of PTSD during their lifetimes. It's an intrinsic and universal part of the human experience. The causes may range from a tragic accident, the unexpected death of a loved one, the onset of a life-threatening illness, or long-term abuse. In general, any type of severe, stress-inducing event has the potential to cause PTSD.

Particularly among young adults, lesser emotional events or acts may trigger PTSD. Classic examples for teenagers include bullying or "body shaming." These can lead to a variety of pathological symptoms and, in some cases, to clinical depression or suicide.[1]

One example of large-scale trauma is the forced relocation of American Indian tribes to government-run areas. The tribe members had never experienced the compulsory labor that came with this involuntary move, and the results of this trauma are still playing out among many American Indians to this day. Sadly, the world is full of similar examples of mass trauma on non-combatants, causing many people to live in intolerable conditions (or risk trying to escape).

Science and its medical counterparts, including psychotherapy, have become deeply involved in analyzing and treating humans with severe cases of trauma. *The Body Keeps the Score* by Dr. Bessel Van Der Kolk, M.D., provides a tour de force about trauma and the post-trauma treatment patterns which have been developed over time.

Dr. Van Der Kolk concludes that no single healing modality fits all when it comes to each individual's recovery, and he confirms that combat-related PTSD has proven particularly difficult to remediate.

## Recognizing the Gap

When it came to Navy SEALS, mental wellness wasn't ever a topic normally discussed. The overt concern about our health focused largely on maintaining our physical wellness and correcting any behaviors that posed a physical risk to us. Those behaviors—

such as inebriation or fighting—could lead to disciplinary action by the superior in command. And, for the record, we got the blame for many fights, but: "The Marines always started it."

That healthcare gap is obvious, when you consider that combat veterans throughout history have suffered from PTSD. The complexities of the situation may be difficult to understand.

There is no amount of training which fully prepares the psyche for the sights, sounds, and smells of an actual combat zone, whether that be the "kill zone" of a SEAL ambush or the site of combat interactions between larger-sized forces. I would imagine the impact is similar for first responders arriving at the scene of all kinds of atrocities or mayhem. The psychological challenges are inevitable.

But here's the odd thing. A combat environment can actually be thrilling to experience, even as unspeakable events are unfolding. The human psyche can crave this type of stimulation, while at the same time being unable to successfully adjust to the physical and psychological reality that it is absorbing. And, like my friend, many people shuffle overwhelming events into "foxholes" in their minds until something triggers the follow-on effects of the traumatic incidents.

Members of the Armed Forces may be conditioned and trained to kill the enemy in combat, but science tells us that it does not prepare them for the mental anguish many of them experience when they return home.

## Eroding Mental Health

Many veterans report a feeling of listlessness after leaving the armed services, particularly those who experienced combat. The psychological let-down of returning to a more normal existence at home may then be followed by PTSD symptoms. The problem is, combat-related PTSD can often be very resistant to therapies that may work better for other types of this disorder.

In my experience, SEALs returning from combat tours have had a variety of mental reactions, although there was often a lag time for the symptoms to show up. The shock of events can sometimes take years to break through to the surface of the mind, which delays the PTSD diagnosis and the treatment.

Some veterans have remained relatively unaffected by their operational experiences, at least from the outside looking in. Others became more overtly religious or more patriotic. A number of them turned to excessive alcohol use (the drug of choice among deployed SEALs throughout my time in the Navy). And sadly, some went truly crazy in terms of their personal habits, actions, and attitudes.

## Looking at the Spiritual Impact

Often the real tragedy of what occurred and was documented among U.S. members of the armed forces was not simply the psychological and physiological effects of PTSD. Many times, the overall values structure that these individuals possessed going into combat was essentially blown up by what they experienced.

The third leg of that metaphorical, three-legged stool—spiritual well-being—was literally in a state of atrophy.

These veterans left the war at odds with themselves. They often reported having little or no feelings of purpose for their lives and no idea how to go about putting back the pieces of their values structure. This kind of disillusionment is devastating.

As I discovered, the collapse of the values structure is a common problem for many trauma survivors, whether they have been through motor vehicle accidents, violent crimes, childhood sexual abuse, or any other horrific experiences. Some of these victims recover over time without outside intervention. They maintain their original values structure despite the trauma, or they adopt a new and viable one. Unfortunately, the rest often develop formal PTSD symptoms and suffer the consequences of a values structure that is decimated.

From this angle, people suffering from PTSD not only need help to treat the physical symptoms, but also to establish a roadmap that helps them recover a values system in which they can believe. This is a critical issue that can be completely misunderstood or even ignored.

In my opinion, the path to recovery from PTSD often lacks a crucial emphasis on the healing power generated from an actively believed-in spiritual practice.

I certainly suffered from that void during and after my first SEAL deployment. My prior religious beliefs had largely disappeared, and I superficially felt that I was an atheist or an agnostic. As far as I was concerned, the meaning of life—if there was one—was too obscure to comprehend.

In highlighting the importance of the "spiritual" leg of the three-legged stool that each of us stands on, I do not mean to denigrate the value of medicine and science in any way. Doctors and scientists have made great strides in developing effective trauma treatment practices. I simply believe we also must look beyond the purely scientific modalities of treatment when seeking to affect long-term physical and psychological improvement.

One book which does an excellent job of highlighting the spiritual part of the equation is called *Trauma and PTSD* by Cathy Chapman, Ph.D. It provides a deep and comprehensive look at the causes and effects of trauma and PTSD on the energy aspects of our beings, and I highly recommend it.[2]

## Making a Move

After my first SEAL combat tour in Vietnam, I was transferred back to a UDT team in San Diego, California. As Operations Officer, my job was to help prepare the entire UDT command to deploy to the Philippines and, subsequently, to deploy in platoon-sized units to Vietnam, largely for underwater demolition work on various canals and rivers.

Moving from active SEAL duty to UDT was good for me psychologically. My time in Vietnam during this deployment was simply that of an overseer of UDT activities and, except for a few patrols with both UDT and SEAL platoons, I did not feel particularly at risk. The biggest dangers of our activities at this time were booby-traps, which managed to kill or maim several members of my UDT team.

## Taking Time to Reflect

During my initial deployments, things happened so quickly that I hadn't stopped to reflect on the bigger world picture in which I was playing a small part. Returning from Vietnam and the Philippines to the United States, I became directly aware of the acute division of opinions inside the country about our combat activities in Vietnam. At first, I was taken aback by what I perceived as hatred and potential violence against myself and my military service colleagues.

As for me and my fellow SEALs, our initial reaction was a desire to directly confront this perceived threat. One of my close SEAL friends painted his Volkswagen "bug" in full camouflage, and we began carrying nightsticks in our vehicles for proactive response if anyone wanted to confront us.

That tension prompted me to start focusing more on the background details of why and how our nation had become involved in this war. As our military efforts in Vietnam began to wind down, I came to believe that our initial rationale for being there was erroneous.

My perception became that we had served no fundamentally positive purpose there over the years of combat. Based on my observations, the regime we supported was overtly corrupt, and the majority of Vietnamese people did not want to fight—either for us or for their corrupt government.

During these years, I consumed way too much alcohol. This was not abnormal among team members, and drinking heavily to relieve the psychological and physical stress was the social norm for many of us. It became hard to tell the difference between heavy drinkers and alcoholics.

I was outwardly happy but psychologically unsettled. Something inside me was rebelling against the events that I had experienced in Vietnam, but I also simultaneously reveled in the life of being a Navy SEAL. The emotional discord was sometimes disturbing.

I will say that I lost my desire to ever hunt or kill anything following my years with the SEALs. This is often the case when men have been engaged in hunting or being hunted by other humans. I see nothing wrong with hunting for food, which mankind has done from the beginning of time. But, for me, hunting for fun was not something I wanted to do thereafter.

## Choosing my Next Steps

After five years as an officer, I was seriously considering leaving the Navy because of the promotion requirement ("up or out"). Getting promoted meant I would have to leave SEAL platoon life and take on positions of more responsibility, which I feared would be largely at a desk somewhere.

I interviewed with the Central Intelligence Agency, developed a business plan to buy and run a ski lodge, and started a small import-export company. I also studied for and received a real-estate sales license and formed a company with 22 other SEALs to invest in real estate. At one point, I seriously considered becoming a mercenary soldier for hire in Africa. In short, the future was blurry, but I was casting about with great energy to find a viable, challenging future path in my life.

By incredibly good fortune, I received notice that I was to be awarded an Olmsted Foundation Scholarship to study at any university of my choice.

The scholarship opportunity stood in sharp contrast to all my other options. From my perspective at the time, the downside was that I would owe the Navy two years of service for every year of the scholarship. Essentially that would mean that I would probably want to finish in the Navy until eligible for retirement. But the upsides were tremendous.

In my opinion, the Olmsted Scholarship is one of the finest scholarships on earth, and the former participants were impressive. The roster of past scholars in this program contains many truly distinguished names: Admiral Carlyle Trost, former Chief of Naval Operations; General John Abizaid, former Commanding General of Central Command and U.S. Ambassador to Saudi Arabia; and Robert "Bud" MacFarlane, National Security Advisor to President Reagan.

Each year, three officers from the Army, Air Force, and Navy/Marine Corps are selected and spread out around the globe for their years of study. An Olmstead scholar can pick any curriculum in any university in the world that would accept him or her, with the sole caveat being that studies had to be focused on, and conducted in, the language of the host country.

A second goal of the program was that scholars immerse themselves in the culture of the country and avoid any resident Americans there as much as possible. Full cultural immersion was the goal, as opposed to academic grades, which were considered secondary during the overseas study period.

Additionally, the program offered scholars a chance to obtain a formal advanced degree by attending the university of their choice in the United States for one final year. In my case, I subsequently returned to the U.S. and enrolled in the University of Oklahoma, ultimately receiving an M.A. and Ph.D. there.

I cannot speak too highly about the value of the Olmsted Scholarship for participating officers. It was (and still is) simply a unique opportunity for personal and professional growth.

## Moving to Madrid

I made the decision to accept the scholarship in 1972, and it essentially changed the way I looked at life from that point on. I chose to take six months of language training in Spain prior to enrolling at the University of Madrid.

From the moment I arrived in Spain, I felt an overwhelming sense of freedom. It was a huge relief, and I sensed a real joy of life there. I had been in a rigorous military environment for the previous ten years, and I hadn't fully recovered psychologically from my combat experiences. This release from structure was good for me at every level.

I immediately rented a bed in a student dormitory, and I let my hair grow (literally and figuratively) to blend in with the local culture at the university. I quickly met a Spaniard named Juan Carrasco. He was about my same age, and we became lifelong friends. Three years later, I was the best man at his wedding, and we remained close until he died in 2017.

My time in Spain allowed me to begin the decompression process that was critical for me after my combat experiences. As the cultural immersion kicked in, I noticed that my thoughts and dreams alternated between English and Spanish. At times, this made me feel as though I had two different personalities: my American self who saw life and my role too seriously; and my Spanish self who was almost always in a good mood with a "carpe diem" attitude.

Perhaps I would be one of the lucky ones who could successfully filter out the negative impact of war and come out psychologically sound. Or maybe not.

## Seeing the Damage

I had been living in Spain for less than a month, and one day I was driving across Madrid on a main boulevard. I wasn't sure exactly where I was supposed to turn, but I pulled up into what would be considered the right lane. At this time in Spain, there were no lane markings or turn indicators. Frankly, Spaniards drove around with what I called "jungle rules."

While I was stopped at the red light, I realized that I needed to continue straight ahead to reach my destination, rather than turning. A taxi driver pulled up behind me and immediately began laying on his horn. I put my hands up in the air and tried to indicate I couldn't move until the light changed. The honking continued.

Finally, the light did change, and I proceeded directly ahead. I suddenly realized the taxi driver had followed me through the intersection rather than turning right, which he urgently wanted to do just a few seconds before. He pulled up alongside my car, recognized I was a foreigner, and rolled down his right-side window to continue berating me. I tried to explain to him what I was doing in Spanish by shouting out my window, but he wouldn't stop harassing me.

The frustration took over, and I slammed on my brakes to stop. I briefly put my head down against the steering wheel. But when I looked up, I realized that the taxi driver had also stopped about 75 yards ahead of me. He had gotten out of his taxi and was headed back toward me.

At this point, I lost complete control of my anger.

I swung open my door, got out, and began running full speed toward the man with the intention of beating him senseless. Obviously, there was no doubt about what I was prepared to do. The taxi driver quickly ran back to his vehicle and sped off before I could reach him.

I turned back toward my car and began shaking uncontrollably, realizing I had overreacted in a shocking way. When I thought about the act I had almost committed, I was stunned. Where did that come from?

I relate this now only because this incident was the catalyst that started me on a search to find my true self and the purpose for my life. It was a turning point. Later, I came to understand that a complete overreaction to subsequent minor stimulus is an often-reported reaction of military service members with PTSD.

It took some time to show up, but I had not escaped it.

***<u>Notes:</u>***

1. Overwhelming clinical medical evidence of the physical and psychological benefits of an active spiritual practice on young children and teens is extremely clearly presented by Lisa Miller, Ph.D., in her books *The Spiritual Child* and *The Awakened Brain*, Picador Publishers, multiple years.
2. Chapman, Cathy, Ph.D., *Trauma and PTSD*, Light Technology Publishing, Flagstaff, Arizona, 2020. Any major trauma also has a direct effect on the emotional body, or limbic part of the brain; in other words, the parts of the brain that are below the "thinking brain" parts. Rebalancing and healing this aspect of our being involves dealing with the energetic aspects of our being. Chapman's book provides a roadmap on approaches to address this aspect of trauma.

# CHAPTER 7
# THE STRUGGLE TO MOVE ON

*"If you are going through hell, keep going."*
**—Winston Churchill**

Following my early years as a SEAL, my mind was occupied with digesting the things that I had experienced and done.

Nothing truly prepares a person for taking another human's life, and the psyche reacts to these events in ways that cannot be predicted prior to the experiences. The psychological reaction also extends to scenes that are witnessed in a combat environment, even if an individual wasn't personally involved.

The after-effects of trauma can be analyzed in stages, although that's rarely helpful for people in the midst of severe PTSD symptoms. Sometimes all that is possible is simply showing up and getting through each day as best they can. But, on some level, there's hope in knowing that both the mind and the body will adjust over time—although it's possible the effects of severe grief never completely disappear.

Patience is required even though the perceived symptoms may seem overwhelming. People do have the capacity to move to the far end of the phases.

## Mental Withdrawal

In terms of my personal symptoms, I found myself in an initial period of mental and spiritual uncertainty and withdrawal, which seemed to impact many of us as SEALs. I could see it most clearly in cases where a friend's physical injuries were severe. Withdrawal is a natural human reaction, just like when someone is given the diagnosis of a terminal disease. You just emotionally pull inside yourself while you try to make sense of something that will never actually make sense.

This initial adjustment period is unavoidable and necessary, but the challenge is to not get stuck in this phase. If a person cannot move past this point, they remain confused, often despondent, and overwhelmed by the challenges.

During this phase, trauma victims may fail to find any bigger purpose or meaning behind the tragic event (or events) they've experienced, and that needs to be seen as acceptable. Far too many people with PTSD are reluctant to seek help, perhaps because they think others can't really understand what they've been through. They also dread someone else trying to interpret their pain and tie it up neatly with a bow. It's messy, and it doesn't work that way.

If you are in this situation, I want to encourage you to seek help—from friends, loved ones, or qualified professionals. There is absolutely no disgrace in that. Be kind and patient with yourself, and recognize there are people out there who can provide the support you need.

## A Sense of Direction

In my case, the second phase of healing began in Spain, where I started to discover a sense of spiritual direction for my life that I could follow for reasons that I will discuss. The events during this period led to a course of action I had faith in. I've always felt like a student, and I suddenly had a whole new field to study. Of course, I didn't have all the answers, but I had a bunch of serious questions.

I also began to understand the importance that an individual's beliefs hold in triggering his or her emotions, thoughts, and actions. I certainly came to realize that my overall belief structure and innate spiritual nature needed conscious strengthening.

This is a complex subject for further discussion, but I just want to make this point up front: What you believe about yourself, your life, your actions, your origin as a human, your religion, and your race are often beliefs that you hold *without ever examining them as such.* Sometimes they are just lodged in the mind like an automatic, unconscious default rather than an acknowledged state or a specific choice.

Here are a few examples.

Maybe you believe that life is "a vale of tears," and we all must struggle. Or your belief system says we are born "sinners" and must take actions to save ourselves. Perhaps you believe it is better to be white than black; or male rather than female; or rich instead of poor—or the exact opposite of any of those. But whatever fundamental beliefs you hold affect your physical, mental, and emotional reactions to life's events as they occur.

The interesting thing is, every belief we hold can be changed, but only if we consciously examine it. So, if we are having disturbing physical and emotional symptoms, what keeps us from analyzing our beliefs and changing those that don't serve us? I'll share some of the primary reasons.

## Three Belief Paradigms

For most of us born in what is referred to as the "Western World" of the Americas and Europe, we are all directly affected by three major belief paradigms of our culture.

First, science has largely defined what we believe to be real. A fundamental tenet of science is that life basically is accidental. We exist because of an evolutionary struggle that led to mankind, which has no transcendent reason for being and no future after each individual's death. So why look for divine meaning when there is none?

Second, religious traditions of the multiple branches and sects of Christianity posit man as a "sinner" requiring baptism for spiritual birth. Christians are then expected to follow the dictates of the dogma of whatever branch of Christianity they are part of. The penalty for serious disagreement or probing of dogma within the Roman Catholic Church historically is called "heresy" and regularly resulted in "excommunication" (which was essentially full ostracism), persecution, or death.

So, the historical message has been for followers to just accept the "word" of the church as "gospel" and to be very careful before trying to branch out on their own. The psychological weight that a person carries for believing in being born a sinner because of Adam's "original sin" is largely unrecognized but very real.

Third, beginning primarily with Freud and the advent of modern psychotherapy, there is the widespread belief that people shouldn't delve deeply into their own minds and traumas without trained therapists at hand. The fear is that doing so could put them at risk of falling prey to their lessor natures or other untamed desires discovered inside. From its beginning, psychotherapy has sought be an off-shoot related to science at its core.

With these three interweaving belief structures influencing most of us, it is little wonder that personal exploration of our inner subjective beings has not been popular as a norm.

## Additional Challenges

There's another factor that poses a fundamental challenge to strengthening our spiritual well-being. For all the knowledge that has been gained through science and the scientific method, many (if not most) humans believe that our mind or "intellect" is the primary tool for "figuring things out." We feel that our brains should be able to consider all the options and project into the future whether a current situation is going to get better or worse. Unfortunately, this often leads to a preponderance of negative thoughts about the future.

To complicate matters, we now know that the various parts of the brain look at life and events from very different perspectives.[1] Our intellect or "ego" is primarily a tool for discerning about the direct reality affecting us in each moment as we experience it, and for helping us set and move toward our goals. But the ego does not have the whole picture and is not the sole actor in bringing about the circumstances we encounter.

When the ego feels that it has to find or have all the answers to both personal and world issues, it can and does go into overwhelm. It's just not equipped to act in isolation from the other parts of our human consciousness.

Added to this is a commonly held assumption that anything wrong will get worse. If this were actually the case, our world would not have survived into the present, which is worth remembering.

Lastly, many males are taught not to express emotions that might show weakness or vulnerability because that might distress or disturb people. If boys cry or express fear, they are often told to "quit acting like a girl." In the United States and many other countries, the male role model is a John Wayne type who dislikes emotions and prefers action to explanation. As women assume more traditionally male roles, they may also feel the necessity to imitate the male prototype image in a career or job.

## From Thinking to Feeling

Most of us spend the majority of our lives in our minds. But embarking on a spiritual search requires opening ourselves up to emotions and moving from our minds to also using our hearts. When feeling overwhelmed by negative thoughts, it's helpful to remember that the actual act of thinking is effortless. It is a "miracle" in itself.

The rest of this book will explore how you can overcome these impediments as you embark on your personal, spiritual path.

***Note:***

1. A truly interesting and scholarly work is *The Master and His Emissary*, by Dr. Lain McGilchrist, MD., on how, in the divided human brain (two hemispheres), each side sees the world differently. The two sides are often in conflict, and the left side (rational, sequential picture taking, etc.) regularly overpowers the right side in many people (our "big picture" side, which sees things wholly, with a more panoramic, spiritual and artistic view). Two books by Dr. Jill Bolte Taylor, *My Stroke of Insight* and *Whole Brain Living* are truly astounding reading about her experiences and the functions (and differing "personalities") of the four principal lobe sections of our brains.

# CHAPTER 8
# THE CONSCIOUS SEARCH BEGINS

*"When the student is ready, the teacher will appear."*
**—Lao Tzu, Ancient Chinese Philosopher**

*Why*
*Just show you God's menu?*

*Hell, we are all*
*Starving—*

*Let's*
*Eat!*
**—Hafiz / *The Gift***

At one point following my initial SEAL deployment, someone higher up in the military world decided that Navy SEALs might benefit from hypnosis training to help control pain, or as an aid to sleep. One of our Navy medical officers had some experience with hypnosis, and I somehow found myself in a few sessions with him.

Nothing much came of this, but it did spark my interest in mind-over-matter as a real utility in life. That prompted me to pick up a book called *Powers of Mind* by the American author Adam Smith. He wrote about his travels around the world looking for humans with mental capabilities that were truly "outside the box," as defined by both science and most traditional religions.

The title of his book says it all. Our minds are the key to effective life changes. His ideas were captivating, and this book literally ignited me with thoughts about the extended possibilities of the human mind. I wanted to know more.

While living in Madrid, I somehow obtained a copy of *Journey to Ixtlan* by Carlos Castaneda. This book is purported to be the notes of a Ph.D. candidate from the University of Berkeley in California. Castaneda traveled to Mexico, ostensibly to do research on the native Indian cultures there. In reality, he was looking to get high on peyote or other psychotropic plants. During his travels, he met an old Indian named Don Juan, who was a shaman and quite advanced in his teaching.

In short, the story in this book intrigued me. As I read it, I came across some instructions from the old Indian concerning how to separate your consciousness from your body. As described by Don Juan, part of his tribe had evolved to do this out of necessity shortly after the arrival of the Spaniards in the "new" world of America. This transition created such a psychological and physiological shock to the native populations that they needed a coping mechanism.

Don Juan's tribal culture decided to spend time trying to get into their minds and out of their bodies, rather than accept the new reality in which they found themselves living.

According to Don Juan, getting the mind out of your body for "astral travel" was simply the first step, and it was relatively easy. What was harder was finding yourself where you wanted to be—for example, in the town where you grew up or in a specific house or classroom. And lastly, hardest of all was making time move by seconds and minutes normally while in your astral body. Once you were there at this highest level, you essentially had two parallel existences simultaneously.

Don Juan was describing out-of-body experiences (OOBEs), under the broader term "metaphysics." There is voluminous literature on this subject by OOBE participants, available to anyone who is interested. The fact is, we are biologically equipped for OOBEs, which allow a certain portion of our consciousness to leave our bodies and then return. The tribe members had perfected it.

To be clear, it is not my intention to argue about the validity of OOBEs with anyone who has a different opinion on the subject. I am fully aware that neither the Western world's versions of most religions nor modern science per se is ready to admit to the reality of OOBEs. I will say this position becomes almost comical when discussing OOBEs with those who have actually experienced them. In addition, it should be noted that both the U.S. Government and the Soviet Union/Russian Government have spent large amounts of money and efforts in the area of human OOBEs and paranormal capabilities for many years, while keeping their respective results secret.

## Pursuing Out-Of-Body Experiences

In a spirit of simple exploration and adventure, I began following the instructions for astral travel in the book by Castaneda. I set out to understand the utility and import of this phenomenon for myself. Within a relatively short period of possibly two weeks or so, I had my first OOBE.

Besides being spectacularly interesting, OOBEs were the gateway that led me to begin rebuilding the spiritual leg of my three-legged stool. The experiences awakened in me a new sense of wonder and an enthusiasm to know more about how OOBEs are possible. Not knowing where to turn for more guidance, I finished the Castaneda series of books and continued with my OOBEs whenever they occurred.

I can say, without a doubt, these experiences dramatically changed my perspective about life and reality.

When first achieving full conscious volition in an OOBE (the ability to act with free will and the consciousness you use when awake), I felt like I was grabbing my spirithood and creaturehood simultaneously with both hands, so to speak. I had an overwhelming sense that each of those had a far greater reality than I had previously supposed. I suddenly felt like I was in a scene from *The Wizard of Oz*, in which Dorothy says to her little dog: "Toto, we're not in Kansas anymore."

What can be said about such an experience?

My religious background to this point had been more about listening to the spiritual words but never actually feeling the impact. To paraphrase the English mystic Alan Watts: Nobody ever got wet from the word *water*. My experiences with OOBEs were the exact reverse. I was actually swimming in the water, and all my senses were fully alive.

In my early OOBEs, the simple joy and adventure of achieving this state with all my senses active (and having normal, conscious decision-making capability) was my primary goal. Each new OOBE provided new stimulus. I found that learning to operate in an OOBE environment is somewhat similar to children learning to experience themselves in life through walking, talking, and accumulating knowledge about the world. It's a skill that improves with practice.

In a full OOBE, my senses are completely alive and functioning. This is in stark contrast to what may be the case while I am "awake"—half asleep or dormant because of being tired, just having eaten, being older, or otherwise not fully alert. Those physiological sensations disappear. This means that colors and smells and other sense impressions can almost be overwhelming in their purity and beauty.

I soon learned that sexual instincts can be equally stimulated. Following the advice of another OOBE practitioner, I found that stopping to explore my sexual urges could bring a quick end to the OOBE. My sensory sensations could soon become overwhelming, forcibly waking me up back in my bed and out of the OOBE experience. So, the best method for me was just to keep moving in the OOBE and tell myself that I would return to that scene later. This has worked for me, generally, and allowed my OOBEs to continue.

Other incredible things can be experienced in OOBEs, such as flying or levitating. For example, in various OOBEs, I practiced take-offs and landings. In at least one instance, I found myself going so fast through outer space that I became worried about my ability to return to my body. This caused me to immediately jolt fully awake, back in my bed.

Some OOBEs occur just a few feet above your sleeping body in your bedroom. The first sight of yourself—sound asleep below—can be quite a shock. It is also possible to levitate up through the top of your house and look down on the roof from above it.

The mechanics of my OOBEs followed a normal routine. I would become wide awake in a normal dream scene where normally I've never been conscious of before. Then I would experiment with complete conscious volition as I move about and encounter people and events in this locale. When I am ready to exit the OOBE, I simply move any part of my body (e.g., hands, fingers, feet, toes) and come immediately back to full consciousness in bed.

Based upon an analysis of astral travel and OOBEs of various natures, it is my belief that most everyone has an OOBE period regularly at night. However, if you go from a dream to a conscious OOBE and then back to a normal dream before waking, you wake up without conscious knowledge of your OOBE.

By going directly from the OOBE to a wide-awake state in bed, you bring the full conscious knowledge of the OOBE back with you. Then I normally get out of bed and write the experience down while it is fresh, before going back to sleep.

It took the reality of OOBEs to alert me to the fact that there was more to "reality" than I had previously thought. I then began a conscious effort to find out more about this phenomenon, which led me directly to various metaphysical authors. Ultimately, I came to the realization that OOBEs have a clearly spiritual message: Despite what science and religion say, we are NOT tied to our bodies!

This personally experienced knowledge provides an intense relief from a preoccupation with dying. Simply put, our consciousness is present before our birth, during our lives, and after we die.

Over the years, my long-term interest in OOBEs led me to meet numerous people who shared their own experiences with me. A couple of simple encounters will illustrate the point.

## Highlighting Other Examples

While in the Navy on a road trip to a SEAL training site, I was assigned a Navy enlisted driver whose job was to get me there. The driver saw my book on OOBEs, which was lying on the seat of the car between us.

After some discussion, this sailor admitted to having OOBEs intermittently since he was about 13 years old. During these episodes, he would find himself being about four feet above his body and looking down on it while walking. He admitted that these experiences terrified him, since he had no background knowledge about OOBEs. As we talked about the universality of this phenomenon throughout history by individuals who have discussed and/or written about it, he became a lot more comfortable with the thought of having these occurrences in the future.

Some years later while attending the Senior Naval War College in Montevideo, Uruguay, I was getting a haircut at the U.S. Embassy barbershop. The barber was 90 years old and deaf, so his granddaughter was there to communicate the needs of the client to the barber using sign language and lip reading to him in Spanish. Again, I must have had a book about OOBEs with me that prompted a conversation.

The granddaughter and I chatted about it for a couple of minutes. She then told me that, two years earlier, she had a hysterectomy. While under anesthesia, she found herself out of her body and wide awake.

She became bored with staying in the room along with her body, so she set out to explore the building. Being on their equivalent of social security, she was not allowed to know the name of the doctor doing the surgery. But, while out of her body, she saw and recognized him while he was doing the procedure on her.

Upon regaining consciousness, she explained her experience about watching the doctor and looking around the building. When the nurse showed great confusion and concern, she became afraid they would label her as crazy. She said that she had never told anyone about this incident since that time, except me.

## Experiencing It on Your Own

For anyone interested in personally experiencing an OOBE, you can easily experiment by taking the following steps.

When settling in to take a nap or before going to sleep at night, clear your mind and then tell yourself (giving a simple instruction to your mind) that sometime during the nap/night you will find yourself looking at your hands in a normal dream. The action of seeing your hands will bring you wide awake in the dream scene.

When this happens, keep your hands in your OOBE up in sight of your eyes to maintain your awake focus in the scene. Your hands act like a focal point for your consciousness. This focus of attention allows you to have full voluntary cognition in the scene, consciously controlling your thoughts and movements.

This process is similar to learning how to walk. One step at a time. With practice, you will get more comfortable and competent at maintaining a full volitional focus. Tell your body in bed to relax and stay asleep. Often the excitement of waking up inside your dream will wake your sleeping body up, which is not what you want.

When you are ready to leave the scene, move any part of your sleeping body in bed. Your hand, leg, or foot are easy parts you can command to move. This movement will bring you back to fully wide awake in bed.

I recommend you get up and write the episode down. If the conditions are such that you can have one OOBE, you can probably have several if you want to. I've also found, for whatever reason, it is easier to have an OOBE if the couch or bed upon which you are lying is oriented in a north-south direction, rather than east-west.

After you have had a successful experience, or if you have tried the above without success for several weeks, I strongly recommend reading about OOBEs from any reputable source.

To reiterate, giving your mind a direct instruction before going to bed or taking a nap that this is what you want it to do while in a dream may be the most important part of all this. It's similar to giving the mind instructions about any problem or challenge in your life that you want it to work on while you are asleep. Otherwise, the mind operates like a computer which may randomly select its own programs for the sleep periods.

There are two major issues to understand about this topic. First, your beliefs may be a major factor in either allowing or keeping you from having an OOBE. For example, if you believe that it is unsafe, morally wrong, or impossible, you may prevent yourself from having the experience. Consider whether these beliefs need to be examined and either reinforced or replaced with more supportive beliefs.

Second, the actual mechanics of body exit and reentry need to be understood. It's helpful to know which physical situations and conditions enhance the likelihood of an OOBE. Your chance of having a positive experience increase if you know the basic "rules of the road." Learning the basics is just common sense, as you would with any skill like downhill skiing or playing the violin.

I will recommend several introductory resources in the Appendix of this book.

Although the advent of OOBEs in my life ignited my interest in understanding myself from a broader perspective and led to my subsequent interest in the importance of spirituality to every person, I want to be clear that OOBEs are not at all necessary to begin a more active spiritual journey. Any activity, incident, or practice such as meditation or active prayer can foment the desire to go on an active spiritual path for more personally meaningful spiritual understandings.

Simply put, true spirituality is all about love. Everything else is just "window dressing."

### Exploring the Link to Dreams

Before moving on, I want to briefly discuss the topic of dreams and dreaming. My early life experiences with dreams would be considered pretty normal by my standards at the time. Growing up, I recall having some vivid dreams and an occasional "bad" dream in which I was being chased or otherwise in a situation I considered extremely dangerous. Upon waking, I didn't remember any significant carry-over effects in my life.

After I began experiencing OOBEs, my interest in dreams increased. The majority of my OOBEs start in a normal dream situation, so I saw the importance of taking notes about my dreams. From there, I became more systematic in my research and understanding of dreams from the perspectives of various spiritual teachers. I knew that dreams were the subject of quite a bit of purely scientific work, but I didn't find anything that really surprised me.

On the other hand, I was intrigued by the perspectives of many spiritual and metaphysical teachers who discussed the importance of dreams and dreaming to the human psyche. I particularly recommend *Edgar Cayce on Dreams* by Harmon Bro and Hugh Lynn Cayce, as well as *The Psyche: It's Human Expression* and *Dreams and Projections of Consciousness,* both by Jane Roberts. They share extensive insights within these books, but I want to share a few highlights.

According to these teachers and authors, dreams can provide (among other things) a doorway to diverse kinds of knowledge that the human brain/mind combination has access to—including things such as telepathy, clairvoyance, and precognition. These types of information have all received serious scientific study and can be utilized both consciously and unconsciously.

Some information can relate to probable future events in our lives. Other dream aspects can provide information concerning our bodies and current or projected issues affecting us physically. Focused attention to a problem, challenge, or interest area can provide dream insight leading to appropriate actions or creations.

Many humans have used this technique to help solve dilemmas in their scientific, business, or personal activities. Some dreams are simply the mind's computer randomly running a program, since it hasn't received any specific instructions. Dreams also essentially keep life from becoming "closed-ended" by providing sources of information not available to the waking state. Many creators and inventors report this latter benefit of dreams.

Webster's dictionary defines "psyche" as the human soul, mind, or spirit. In essence, we are our psyche's living expression, its human manifestation. The psyche can also be described as a gestalt of aware energy having a human focus. When we sleep, our dreaming psyche is awake. It simply has a different focus.

The American mystic Jane Roberts describes it well:

*"Your 'dreaming' psyche seems to be dreaming only because you do not recognize that particular state of awareness as your own. The 'dreaming' psyche is actually as awake as you are in your normal waking life. The organization of wakefulness is different, however. You come into dreaming from a different angle, so to speak."*[1]

This is a fascinating topic to explore, but it boils down to this: Our psyches can and do operate in different modes, but our individual beliefs about reality and the nature of sanity can and do often inhibit or censor the learning experiences which are available to us in dreams. By insisting that our "dreaming" psyche follow the norms of our waking psyche, we have trouble making sense of our dream recollections. The truth is, the dimensions of our psyche need to be experienced. They cannot be simply defined.

I began keeping notebooks to record my dreams, and I have continued this practice for many years. Over time, I realized that I have received information in each of the categories I mention above. And almost every one of my life's major decisions has been assisted by dream information.

As with any skill, consciously utilizing dream information requires some simple techniques and practice. We can easily have such a limited idea of the capabilities of our personhood that we discount or ignore anything beyond those parameters. The key to expanding that view is to first accept these other states of consciousness as being native to our psyches and their human counterpart, our brains.

***Note:***

1. Roberts, Jane, *The Nature of the Psyche: Its Human Expression*, Amber-Allen Publishing, California, 1995, p. 18.

# CHAPTER 9
# FINDING MY DIRECTION

*"Courage starts with showing up and letting ourselves be seen."*
**—Brené Brown**

Another life milestone event occurred while I was living in Spain: I met my future wife Heather on a skiing trip to Andorra. Heather was working as a teacher at the British Council School in Madrid, teaching Spanish students to study and speak in English under the British-style educational system. From this point on, *my* life's journey was *our* lives' journey. I had never before known the importance of having a life partner who would give me such unconditional love and support.

Based on my background, you can imagine I was not easy to reach emotionally. My path back to what might be called a healthy emotional basis for giving and receiving love has been a progressive endeavor for us both. Happily married since 1975, I still feel so lucky to have met Heather how and when I did.

Heather's experiences as the wife of a career Navy SEAL could be a separate book altogether. It simply takes a truly exceptional and strong woman to marry (and to stay married to) a Navy SEAL. In fact, any spouse of a deployed military person deserves special mention and credit.

The resilience and competence required of the non-military spouse are nothing short of incredible, and Heather was a prime example. Over the years, we had to come and go, often without notice as to where we were going, what we would be doing, how long we would be there, or when we would be home.

It was also difficult dealing with the physical and emotional state of a SEAL returning home after combat. Many military families would confirm this statement: When the absent spouse returns from a long deployment, particularly one involving combat, the husband-wife relationship often undergoes a radical change. Navigating the changes which have occurred to both participants in a marriage following this type of separation requires love, courage, and flexibility.

## Returning to SEAL Work

I spent the final year of my Olmsted Scholarship at the University of Oklahoma. At the end of this time, I had finished all the course work and general examinations for a Ph.D., and was only lacking the Ph.D. final dissertation. Heather came over to join me permanently from Spain and we were married in Houston, Texas. So immediately following our honeymoon, Heather and I began a frantic month of research and interviews in various cities, collecting material for the dissertation.

This bordered on the comical, since while I was selecting, reading and bookmarking needed documents all day every day,

Heather was spending her time every day running back and forth with a large bag of coins, utilizing the public photocopy machines in the various university libraries while photocopying each of the bookmarked pages in the books, so that I could do the actual writing in the Philippines, our first duty station together as newlyweds. Actually, writing the dissertation didn't seem too arduous at this point.

We arrived in the Philippines in 1975, and I immediately assumed duties as Officer in Charge of all SEAL units in the Western Pacific, for the next three years. This was a chaotic time in that part of the world, as our country began and completed its withdrawal from Vietnam, and the rest of that part of the world remained very unstable. With training and operations simultaneously ongoing in multiple countries in this region, my units were in constant motion.

My first year there turned into a truly stressful personal marathon. I came to feel like I had finally reached true load limit. Working on completing my dissertation required that I get up at 3 AM every morning to work four hours on it before going to work at 7 AM. Returning home in the evenings when no crisis kept me at the office meant arriving around 6 PM. This was the equivalent to working from 8 AM to midnight six days a week, while also being newly married. This went on for over a year, until I finally finished the dissertation.

I mention this simply to make a point. I don't believe that a person should judge any endeavor while being in the midst of it. Whether it be graduating from school, SEAL training, running a marathon, or deciding on undergoing any type of training or job. The time to do the judging about whether you would ever do it again, or not, is after you have finished and collected the experience and whatever recognition ensues from the effort.

The 20-mile mark of a 26-mile marathon is the worst place from which to judge one's efforts.

The reality is that often the personal value of an experience isn't immediately apparent, and often only shows up some time, even years, later in life. This can particularly be true for events or experiences initially seen as negative.

After finishing and defending the dissertation and receiving the Ph.D. degree, Heather and I celebrated by our first real vacation as a married couple. We took a week and went to Borneo to climb the huge mountain there named Kota Kinabalu.

## Continuing my Spiritual Journey

A pivotal event occurred to me in 1979 that highlighted a personal spiritual path forward for me. I was spending a year in Uruguay as a student at the Senior Naval War College in Montevideo.

In addition to me, the class included seven senior Uruguayan officers and one Taiwanese officer. Heather and I loved Montevideo and Uruguay, and I became good friends with the members of my class.

During that year, I continued exploring my OOBEs as they occurred. Then, the fiancée of a Navy friend gave me a copy of the book, *Seth Speaks: The Eternal Validity of the Soul,* by the American author and mystic Jane Roberts.[1] This book and the ones she wrote later have had a profound influence on me. Reading these books opened my mind to the idea that OOBEs had a spiritual lesson for me and for humanity in general. I will discuss this in some detail.

I was assigned as Commanding Officer of SEAL Team One in San Diego after returning from Uruguay. Besides deploying SEAL platoons to various parts of the globe, I became involved in developing a cold-weather training manual for SEAL operations in arctic and sub-arctic environments.

While in Alaska for training operations, I hired a scientist to perform sample tests concerning cold-water exposure on a SEAL's abilities to function mentally and physically over time. On my last night in Alaska, I invited the scientist to dinner.

During our discussions, he mentioned another study he recently completed on the effects of cold-water exposure. He conducted a survey of people who had been revived after near-death experiences, mainly after escaping from drowning or accidental electrocution.

He interviewed about 75 subjects, and he said some of their comments really startled him. He also reiterated that he was just a scientist and not a religious person.

An overwhelming number of those he interviewed remembered OOBEs while they were in a coma, with many describing how they felt guided or compelled to return to consciousness to complete their tasks as humans. He added that the overall experience of drowning and being brought back to consciousness was considered by many to be one of the most significant spiritual experiences of their lives.

Overall, they reported a sense of great peace and certainty with their experience. Later research has shown me that this phenomenon is extremely well documented by other sources.[2]

## Moving to Key West

The Navy next led Heather and me to Key West, Florida, where I served on a joint military staff with service personnel from all four military branches: Army, Navy, Air Force, and Marine Corps. My job at this time was Director of Plans, meaning I developed both war plans and disaster-relief plans for the area. Since the countries of the Caribbean Basin are all hurricane disaster prone, I visited almost all the islands during my tour of duty.

Life in Key West was most agreeable. My first order of business was to get a bicycle as my mode of transportation to and from work. On the way, I always rode past Ernest Hemingway's house. This prodded me to re-read all his books, which I thoroughly enjoyed.

In many ways, Key West hadn't changed much since Hemingway's time. The main two industries were fishing and the Navy. Today, tourism completes the triad of work opportunities, but we were there prior to the advent of cruise ship port visits and streets bustling with people on vacation.

## Lost at Sea

While we were living in Key West, I had an experience that significantly highlighted my changed perspective.

A friend and I co-owned a 24-foot sailboat named "The Happy Heather," and we used it for diving and exploration trips in the Florida Keys. The boat slept four people comfortably, with a cabin, galley, and "head" facility. It had a small outboard motor for docking and mooring or for short trips around the island. I enjoyed this boat immensely.

Two friends and I were on a three-day trip to the island of Dry Tortugas, off the Florida coast, where the prisoner John Wilkes Booth was kept after shooting President Lincoln. On the way home, we detoured off the main sea routes to dive on a specific underwater reef we knew about.

Even though we arrived at the site in the late afternoon, we decided to dive anyway. Then I proceeded to make three poor choices which could easily have cost me my life.

First, we decided all three of us would dive at once, leaving no one on the boat to monitor the situation. Second, being the most experienced diver, I went out on my own and paired the other two men together. That would allow them to go up-current along the reef and return to the boat down-current. I went the other way by myself, which meant I would be returning to the boat against the current. Lastly, one of my friends had a malfunctioning life jacket, so I gave him mine. I used a spare one which didn't have the normal "safety signaling" devices of a flare and whistle.

While underwater away from the boat, I realized that the current was getting stronger. I had been diving for a half-hour and had speared some fish. I decided to turn around and head back underwater toward the boat.

The force of the current had increased significantly, and I was soon reduced to hand crawling forward from rock to rock on the bottom. Getting low on air, I finally surfaced and realized I was still several hundred yards away from the boat. My two friends were back aboard the sailboat, admiring the fish they had speared. I tried shouting and waving, but they were paying no attention. I was only a small visual target, bobbing in the water.

It was getting dark. Despite my best efforts to swim against the current, my distance from the boat kept increasing. Once my friends finally did become alarmed by my absence, they didn't have many options. This was before the era of cell phones, and The Happy Heather didn't have a radio to call for Search and Rescue assistance.

Further compounding the problem, the current had pulled the boat's anchor deep into the reef rock, and it wouldn't release. Rather than simply cutting the anchor loose, they decided one of them would put the scuba gear back on and dive down to the anchor while the other maneuvered the boat in an effort to break free. All this took time.

Darkness fell. I was in a truly strong current stream, and I had lost all sight of the sailboat. My scuba gear and the fish were weighing me down, so I ditched them.

The chances of being found in the darkness were slim. I was sixty miles from the nearest land and didn't expect many boat transits in this area, even in daytime.

Barring a shark attack during the night, I knew I had a day or so before the sun beating down on my head and the lack of water would make me largely incapable of helping myself. My fate was out of my control.

During the hours that I was being carried by the current, I had time to go over the events of my life. I realized that I had been truly blessed. And while I didn't like the thought of how I might meet my demise, I discovered I had no fear whatsoever of dying. I felt calm and only modestly concerned.

About four hours after I had started my dive, The Happy Heather appeared out of nowhere in the darkness. Having finally freed the anchor, my friends did exactly the right thing. They allowed The Happy Heather to drift with her bow down-current. Then they just touched the motor lightly to add a slight extra momentum before going back to drifting down-current, meaning they were on my same drift path. This procedure took them awhile to catch up to me, but it worked.

Looking back at that time, I can see that the spiritual leg of my three-legged stool was, once again, balanced and strong. It was absolutely human and acceptable to be concerned about any given method of dying. But to be completely serene about death is a function of a person's robust spiritual supporting beliefs.

***Notes:***

1. The works of Jane Roberts and Robert Butts have become classics in the fields of psychology and personal growth, as I will discuss in some detail.
2. See, for example, Kubler-Ross, Elizabeth, *On Death and Dying*, Celestial Arts, 2008. Kubler-Ross was a renowned expert on the subject of aging and dying, and she was one of the pioneers in the creation of the hospice movement. In her work, she interviewed over 20,000 dying individuals and came to some remarkable conclusions about the near-death and after-death experiences of humans.

# CHAPTER 10
# SCIENCE AND SPIRITUALITY

*"Man is the most insane species. He worships an invisible God and destroys a visible nature, unaware that this nature he's destroying is this God he's worshipping."*
**—Nova 2023**

When the United States invaded Grenada in 1983, I headed the initial disaster-relief team on the island. This work involved around-the-clock efforts to help sort through the myriad of issues that needed immediate attention. We did everything from rounding up local officials for meetings and arranging flights for necessary items like medicines, milk, and diapers, to paying people to pick up dead bodies off the streets and deliver them to the morgue.

My team was also responsible for drafting the initial damage report which went all the way up to our national command authority. I found this work to be extremely satisfying. It felt rewarding to focus all our efforts on helping to mitigate the effects of this short but violent military action, rather than being part of the units creating the chaos.

After three years in Key West, I worked directly for the head of the Chief of Naval Operations (CNO) as a member of a Navy Strategic Studies Group. Following this tour, I once again reported to the CNO as part of his personal staff in Washington, D.C., involved in long-range planning issues. In the middle of this tour of duty, I was ordered back to the Norfolk, Virginia, area to take command of SEAL Team Six.

Through all these transitions, I continued to sense that my spiritual well-being was undergoing a transformation. I also began exploring the fascinating intersections between science and spirituality.

## Proving the Power of Spirituality

Medical science can now prove beyond reasonable doubt that people of all age groups who are actively engaged in a spiritual journey through life have measurable physiological changes in their brains. Longitudinal medical-research studies—peer reviewed and fully controlled—are unambiguous in showing that these individuals have better results in dealing with such issues as addiction, depression, suicidal urges, and general stress.

Books called *The Spiritual Child* and *The Awakened Brain* by clinical psychologist Dr. Lisa Miller and her colleagues at Columbia University provide overwhelming evidence about the beneficial effects on humans who have what Dr. Miller refers to as a "high-spiritual brain." This means they are actively interested in their personal spiritual growth as they go through life, in contrast with those who have a "low-spiritual brain."

The latter category applies to anyone who doesn't participate in any particular spiritual practice or merely subscribes to some type of religion as a formality without letting it influence their lives in any significant way. Following these classifications, the physical changes to the brain as it grows are astoundingly different.

Reading this material leads to a direct understanding of the importance of spirituality in our lives. No other factor is a greater predictor of overall emotional wellness in normally healthy humans. Active spirituality leads to increased resilience, fewer addictive behaviors, and stronger mental health in individuals.

Suffering can also pull spiritual awareness forward, and it often does. In fact, active spirituality acts like a muscle that we can learn to strengthen. In an awakened brain, there is also a natural capacity to perceive a greater reality.

Anyone interested in the medically documented subject of how spirituality affects mental health issues should take the time to read Dr. Miller's books. Although they largely focus on the psychological and physiological effects of active spirituality on children and teenagers, there is a direct correspondence to the import of these conclusions on PTSD and related trauma cases.

Her conclusions about the connection between mental health and the spiritual leg of our three-legged stools are striking, and I will summarize some of the most important principles here:

- Spirituality is an innate and foundational way of being for each human.
- Spirituality is a muscle that will atrophy or grow strong, depending on whether it is exercised.
- A person's outward goals are no substitute for meaning and purpose.

- The beauty and intricacy of the universe can be a trigger for a belief in God.
- Exercise has a positive effect on the mind, as well as the body.
- Your mind and emotions have a direct effect on your well-being and physical function.
- Spirituality is directly linked to mental health.
- Mind-body-spirit tools can act as "a direct help to navigate fear and doubt and find a path to resilience and renewal."
- Actively spiritual people who believe in a higher power and use this belief daily to help navigate life's challenges have significant physiological and psychological differences compared with those who do not.[1]

This all leads to the concept that a person can be spiritual without being religious—and, of course, the reverse. Active spirituality can be thought of as the link which builds and maintains an interconnection between mind, body, and spirit.

## Integrating Spirituality and Medicine

At one point, I became familiar with a famous American named Edgar Cayce who was born in Hopkinsville, Kentucky, in 1877. Cayce grew up with minimal education and had great difficulties learning in school. He did, however, realize he had certain psychic powers that led him to a 43-year career in *medicine* using his gift of clairvoyance.

Clairvoyance could be defined as a paranormal type of intuition that allows someone to see and perceive things about a person that others cannot. Some might consider it a "sixth sense" that enables the ability to access information from different times and locations.

After reading several biographies about Edgar Cayce, I visited a repository of more than 9,000 microfiche records about his medical cases, which are maintained at the Association for Research and Enlightenment (ARE) library in Virginia Beach, Virginia.[2] I discovered hundreds of complete case reports containing affidavits by patients and documentation by physicians.

Cayce's unique gifts were described in a wonderful biography called *There is a River* by Thomas Sugrue:

> *"He did not use his ability except to prescribe for the sick and to give spiritual advice and vocational guidance when these were specifically requested. He never made any public demonstrations of his powers; he was never on stage; he never sought any publicity; he did not prophesy; he did not seek wealth. Often his economic status was quite precarious; at best, it never rose above modest security. During the period of the Cayce Hospital, he was paid only seventy-five dollars a week for his services."*[3]

As I reviewed his medical files at the ARE library, I noticed that most of the people referred to Cayce had already seen multiple doctors. They had exhausted all the known medical alternatives for their conditions with little or no results.

Cayce's diagnoses came to him while he was in a trance-like state, and the patient outcomes were literally astounding. I was particularly struck by the exact details of physical and psychological issues he could provide for individuals whom he had never met and who often lived in other parts of the United States.

If there was no known drug to treat a particular ailment, Cayce would often dictate the component ingredients and tell people where they could locate them in their various hometowns. Many of these medicinal "recipes" have subsequently been patented by major companies and developed by the pharmaceutical industry.

Cayce was a fundamentalist Christian and vowed to read the Bible cover to cover once for every year of his life. Since he didn't begin this practice until he was around 10 years old, he vowed to read it twice per year until he caught up with his age. Interestingly, he didn't seem to perceive a disconnect between his own spiritual journey and his gift for clairvoyance. As he became more and more comfortable and confident in his abilities, he even agreed to answer questions on other topics besides medicine while in a trance.

Needless to say, given the era in which he lived, Cayce engendered a significant amount of skepticism among the medical and scientific communities, as well as with certain religious officials. Nonetheless, he persevered with his readings and stood by them even when they began discussing concepts like reincarnation and a divinity beyond normal Christian dogma. At this point, he was considered highly controversial by many people—except those who were getting direct benefits from his help.

The Cayce readings and a plethora of books written about the subjects he discussed are all still available. No matter where you are on your own spiritual path, it's impossible to delve deeply into this material without feeling a sense of awe for the source of his information. His work in the field of medicine might have raised plenty of eyebrows, but those 9,000 case files at the ARE library prove the impact he had on countless patients who had run out of options.

If you are interested in more information about the converging paradigms of science and spirituality, there are numerous excellent books including *The Tao of Physics* by Fritz Copra. I think you'll find it fascinating how the outer edges of scientific discoveries continue to get closer and closer to the mystical view of reality as reported by mystics throughout the ages.[3]

## Understanding our Belief Structures

In the chapter on PTSD, I talked about the way trauma can erode a person's values or belief structure. Spiritual leader and author Marianne Williamson wrote about this topic in her book, *A Return to Love*. She explained how her belief structure growing up essentially left her constantly feeling upset, neurotic, guilty, and inadequate. She never felt like she was "good enough."

While this might seem like a normal emotional state for many adolescents and young adults (even high achievers), that feeling can be pervasive and insidious, leading to everything from addictive behaviors to bad life choices. Scientific studies now back this up.

In Williamson's case, she found herself coming out of the emotional fog and redefining her belief structure when she discovered a book called *A Course in Miracles*. She quickly realized it had something important to teach her.[5]

The book's primary authors are Helen Schucman and William Thetford, who were Professors of Medical Psychology at Columbia University's College of Physicians and Surgeons in New York City. The scientists were initially very reluctant to publish material from unscientific sources associated with the topic of miracles, but they saw the value. The introduction to the course set the tone:

> *"This is a course in miracles. It is a required course. Only the time you take it is voluntary. Free will does not mean that you can establish the curriculum. It means only that you can elect what you want to take at a given time. The course does not aim at teaching the meaning of love, for that is beyond what can be taught. It does aim, however, at removing the blocks to the awareness of love's presence, which is your natural inheritance. The opposite of love is fear, but what is all-encompassing can have no opposite."*[6]

Humans all over the world have now benefitted from the teachings about belief structures in this book and are grateful the scientists persevered with their work. As for Williamson, she has used that insight to write a number of wonderful books and to lecture on multiple spiritual topics for worldwide audiences.

In my case, the personal fog began to lift when I started experiencing OOBEs. This type of newfound clarity is literally a personal healing within the psyche, which happens when an individual finds an overarching belief structure that makes sense and feels reliable.

Belief structures can only be seen in their true importance when we understand they form the bedrock foundation of our mental and emotional beings. Our beliefs are not "truths," per se, but simply the repetitive way each of us thinks about ourselves and life, in general.

In addition, beliefs can and do change as we go through life. That means we can consciously adjust and replace beliefs that no longer serve us. In other words, we are not at the mercy of our beliefs unless we choose to leave them unexamined. To feel like we truly have meaning and purpose, we need to first recognize the value of having a viable belief structure. Then we need to mold that construct for ourselves by examining our current beliefs and changing (or eliminating) those that don't suit us.[7]

I was already in the middle of my career as a Naval Officer when I achieved this level of understanding about the importance of belief structures. This allowed me to make positive shifts, adjusting my thoughts and actions more consciously.

Suffice it to say, the spirit leg of the three-legged stool was taking on increasing significance for me. That directly affected my personal decision-making and the way I addressed many of the issues and challenges life would throw at me in the years ahead.

***Notes:***

1. My comments here have been summarized and paraphrased from Miller, Lisa, Ph.D., *The Spiritual Child* and *The Awakened Brain*, Picador and Random House, New York, multiple years.
2. There are many excellent biographies and books describing Cayce's work and conclusions in multiple areas of research of interest to others. As a mystic, Cayce had an incredible gift of diagnosing human medical and psychological ailments, their sources, and the optimum path for healing remediation of symptoms. In many cases, he did all this without ever actually seeing or meeting the subject persons in question.
3. Sugrue, Thomas, *There Is a River,* ARE Press, Virginia Beach, Virginia, 1997, Foreword section.
4. Over the past decades, science has been edging closer to mysticism in search of an understanding of phenomena that don't fit the main scientific paradigms, mainly in the areas of astrophysics and quantum mechanics physics. An excellent book on this subject is Copra, Fritz, *The Tao of Physics,* Shambhala Press, 2010.

5. Williamson, Maryanne, *A Return to Love*, Thorson, 1992, p. xiv.
6. Schucman, Helen and Thetford, William, *A Course in Miracles*, Mill Valley, California, Foundation for Inner Peace, 1992.
7. An overwhelming tour de force highlighting the importance of individual beliefs for humans at all ages is Roberts, Jane, *The Nature of Personal Reality,* Amber-Allen, 2011.

# CHAPTER 11
# THE SPIRITUAL SEARCH

> *"One of the main questions of philosophy: for what may I hope?"*
> **—Emmanuel Kant**

When I look back on it now, my spiritual search was always in progress—even when I wasn't aware of it. I was constantly in the process of unconsciously collecting tidbits of information to either confirm or refute my belief system.

In Vietnam, the atrocities and violence ripped away the foundation of my values structure. But my experiences that followed gave me the spark of curiosity I needed to pursue a spiritual search with more intentionality.

Determining which of our beliefs to keep and which ones to discard is all part of our spiritual search. So, what does that mean exactly? Some people—especially those who crave a more quantifiable approach—find it helpful to give some structure to this ethereal-sounding quest. I want to explore that idea, and I'll start with a parable that offers us both humor and wisdom:

*Ramlogan (the fool) is looking for his house key.*
*A friend comes along and says: "Where did you lose it?*
*Ramlogan: "Over there by my house."*
*Friend: "Then why are you looking for it over here?"*
*Ramlogan: "The light is better over here."*

**—Sufi/Parable**

There's a valuable lesson in that for our personal spiritual search: We have to go where new answers may be found rather than simply staying near the more comfortable, better-lit areas that may no longer hold meaning. Clinging onto our usual, default beliefs out of habit may inevitably leave us feeling stagnant and unfulfilled.

I was starting to understand that on some level. I began to believe that a personal spiritual practice was analogous to brushing my teeth. It's something that should be done daily, and it doesn't have to be a transcendent experience.

## The Spiritual Stages

Years ago, I attended a presentation in San Diego and heard a speaker named Adyashanti, a spiritual teacher devoted to serving the awakening of all beings. He categorized spiritual searches into **four basic stages**.

<u>Stage One</u> is the **basic spiritual urge** which each human is born with. There has been no period of recorded history in which mankind was not searching for life's meaning and for answers about the existence of a divine source. This has resulted in cults and religions believing in multiple gods, in one god, and in a divine creative source without form. But the central fact is, this desire is innate in each human. And it operates like a muscle

that can be strengthened through active practice or allowed to atrophy as a person goes through life.

Stage Two is characterized by **actively searching for ideas to believe in**. This most generally results in the adoption of one religious practice or another.

Stage Three is usually a follow-on phase in which people are **searching for an actual "experience."** In other words, they want to *know* rather than simply read or be preached to about divine truths. This phase is often characterized by meditation, prayer, chanting, or other modalities. It can also be very rigorous and sometimes frustrating for participants.

Stage Four is characterized by **a feeling that we are "ourselves alone."** This thought persists: "I don't even know who I am, much less know enlightenment." At this stage, the ego's fear of the abyss—the leap into nothingness—surges forward. The searcher is left with the understanding that his or her personal trail from this point feels unmarked.

People who reach Stage Four have concluded intuitively that somehow their life matters, but do not yet have the inner certainty that their individuality is not abruptly curtailed at death. Pausing to contemplate this, we remember that there's not much agreement on this topic.

Science posits an abrupt end to our consciousness at death. Many religious sects talk about a heaven in terms of souls in a seemingly mindless adoration of God. And some eastern religious sects believe that, at death, we pass into a type of divine milieu without individuation.

While many people struggle to experience and move through the four general stages of spiritual search, they inevitably keep trying. It's the result of a persistent impulse to continue toward what is seen as an ideal understanding and awareness of our human link to divinity. That drive seems to be universal.

From my perspective, a spiritual search involves simply deciding which beliefs to keep and which to discard. Then we proceed to live life in the present tense, day by day, while continuing our spiritual practices.

## The Human Psyche

One starting premise is that each of us has a "knowing" portion of ourselves which we can understand on a deeper level as we open ourselves to it. This is often referred to as our "psyche"—something that is not physical and cannot be touched or measured. Other terms used to refer to the psyche are soul, mind, entity, inner self, subconscious, or greater being.

In the context of a personal spiritual search, the term *psyche* can simply refer to the composite of these aspects of ourselves which can allow us to explore the broader reaches of creativity and understanding of who we are. It's also the portion of ourselves that allows us to overcome life's adversities and discouragements and, at least momentarily, glimpse a sense of enduring validity to our lives.[1]

But here's the distinction. We may be able to experience the broader dimensions of our human psyche, but we can't describe it in words. The psyche has access to information we don't consciously possess.

As we embark on an optimal spiritual search for ourselves as individuals, we have to start by accepting the rightness of our own personhoods. We each have a right and a reason to be here and to be who we are. If our basic perception of ourselves is "sinful" or unworthy, many of our natural urges to act—our impulses—will seem contradictory or dangerous.

## Our Impulses

As humans, our impulses are the direct communication links from our psyches. Each person is born because of an impulse "to be," which creates and governs the growth of everything from the universes to microbes. If we do not trust the nature of our impulses, then we don't trust the nature of life.

The interaction between our beliefs and our impulses is what leads us to action or non-action. We all have the right to question our impulses to see if they align with our beliefs and understanding of appropriate behavior and, after assessing the options, choose the correct actions for us.

If we investigate our impulses, we often find that many undesirable ones come from frustrated, idealized urges which we feel are beyond our reach or inappropriate for the circumstances. If we fail to act on, or even acknowledge, an impulse or strong feeling again and again, we build up an emotional charge within ourselves. Those bottled-up responses can then be triggered by a relatively minor incident to become a full-scale emotional eruption.

## The Whole Self

Some schools of thought about spiritual development recommend that we minimize or eliminate our mental and physical desires and impulses. This can certainly create a contradiction.

We are intimately familiar with our physical selves, although that part of us is considered notoriously unreliable for giving us insight about our spiritual pathways. On the other hand, we believe that our spiritual self is some seemingly remote inner being that we can trust but can't contact. You can see why these challenges can become impediments to a spiritual search.

For me, author Jane Roberts provides an appropriate understanding:

> *"First of all, the self that you are is ever changing and not static. There is an inner self in terms of those definitions, but that inner self, which is the source of your present being, speaks through your impulses. They provide built-in spiritual and biological impetuses toward your most ideal development. You must trust the self that you are now... If you would know yourself in deepest terms, you must start with your own feelings, emotions, desires, intents and impulses. Spiritual knowledge and psychic wisdom are the natural result of self-unity."*[2]

The reality is, both of these are intertwined and part of our whole being. The inner-self portion of our psyche speaks through our impulses that may become physical actions. We need to remember we are a whole and complete self, worthy of our trust as we continue our spiritual journeys.

***Notes:***

1. Any discussion of the human psyche is inherently complex. One of the most thought-provoking explorations of this central human concept is Roberts, Jane, *The Nature of the Psyche: Its Human Expression*, Amber-Allen Publishing, 1979.
2. Thoughts in this section come from Roberts, Jane, *The Individual and the Nature of Mass Event*s, Amber-Allen, 1995, pp. 295-296. No short synopsis by me can do justice to the ideas presented in this book about the necessity to be a "practicing idealist," meaning to be willing to take small steps towards our ideal goals, and the overall importance of our natural impulses in this regard.

# CHAPTER 12
## METAPHYSICS 101

*"You do not have to fight to trust the thrust of your own life. That thrust is always meant to lead you toward your own best fulfillment, in a way that will benefit the species as well. When you trust the thrust of your own life, you are always supported."*

**—Jane Roberts/Seth**

The personal quest to understand my role in the grand scheme of life led me to discover the principles and teachings of *metaphysics*. For me, this discovery has proven to be a useful guide and support for my life, helping me develop a supportive world view and fueling my spiritual journey.

When I first became aware of the term "metaphysics" and what it represents, I couldn't believe that this whole field hadn't ever been mentioned to me by anyone. This is not actually surprising given the active bias against metaphysics as a path of exploration by science and most active religious traditions.

The term originally came from a series of books written by the ancient Greek philosopher Aristotle.

## Metaphysics Defined

According to the Oxford dictionary, metaphysics is "the branch of philosophy that deals with the first principles of things, including abstract concepts such as being, knowing, substance, cause, identity, time, and space." In simpler terms, it's the study of reality and existence. It's a way of describing the divine source of everything that is and our human situation within it.

A useful point of view in metaphysics is the understanding that each aspect of creation is at the very center of creation. Every human exists as a cause of creation, and not just as an effect of it. And the basic essence of all things is love.

Going beyond conventional religious doctrines and scientific perspectives, metaphysics acknowledges that reality encompasses more than these frameworks can explain. From that angle, it involves a willingness to contemplate that the reality we *think* we know may be way more complex than we previously believed.

***We need a bigger framework.***

Just as the natural order of things in nature requires change and involves growth, so does our innate spirituality. Metaphysics posits that we are in a continual growth mode. If we are open to that constant growth, we can better understand ourselves and our role in life as we experience it.

By seeking to know these physical truths, we eventually discover the spiritual truths of self. And, in that process, it becomes necessary to enlarge the framework from which we view reality.

Studying metaphysics is a way of obtaining a particular outlook on life, beginning from the premise that life has meaning for all of its parts, including all of mankind. I realize that many people do believe that life has meaning. But when they are faced with major obstacles or unexpected trauma, they often become distracted or reject this basic belief. Metaphysics provides perspective in those situations, positioning the human situation in the context of a larger whole.

American author and mystic Jane Roberts, who will be featured in the next chapter, describes it this way:

> *"People have a biologically built-in knowledge that life has meaning. They share that biologically ingrained trust with all other living creatures. A belief in life's meaning is necessary on the part of your species. It is vital for the proper workings of genetic systems. It is a prerequisite for individual health and for the overall vitality of any given 'stock.' Your greatest achievements have been produced by civilizations during those times when man had the greatest faith in the meaningfulness of life in general, and in the meaningfulness of the individual within life's framework."*[1]

## Real-World Applications

Individuals who study metaphysics are asking some bold, thought-provoking questions. For example: How do we fit into the universe? Does God exist? Why is there something instead of nothing? Do we really know what it means to be conscious? What's the meaning of life? Does it matter?

Trying to find those answers has been a human pursuit from the beginning of time. And yet, there are many reasons for a bias against metaphysics, based largely on national cultures and major religious traditions. Those tend to tightly define the parameters of what is considered "right" or appropriate about our existence, leaving little room for personal spiritual exploration.

If you come from one of those backgrounds, I'd like to invite you to read on about metaphysics with an open mind. Simply look at it as a way to broaden your personal understanding of this philosophy. You can absorb the material without completely understanding it or agreeing with it. Just think of it as a resource to expand your knowledge and your horizons.

While metaphysics opened the door to the route on my spiritual journey, I recognize it may not be the right answer for everyone. Any approach which results in an individual realizing the wonder and beauty of life and all of humanity—despite our mistakes and stumbles—is a good road. But this book is about the path I have taken. I hope my story will inspire you to look more deeply into the metaphysical perspective.

Let's begin by examining some of the basic principles involved in metaphysics.

## The Speed of Light

Albert Einstein developed one of the most famous equations of the modern age: $E=mc^2$. While the meaning of this equation and its full implications are only understood by very few people, there's a wealth of information there to be unpacked as we work to dig deeper into metaphysics.

In his equation, Einstein asserts that time slows down as an object approaches the speed of light. That's a complex statement, since the rules we live by simply don't apply at the speed of light or beyond.

Here's how it was described for me by a physics professor. At the speed of light, time as we know it stops. If we had a spaceship capable of traveling at the speed of light, our trip from one end of the universe to the other would be instantaneous.

However, to anyone observing us from earth, 93+ billion years would have passed!

Pause to think about that for a moment. We can understand it intellectually as a concept, but we can't really comprehend it.

This conundrum has caused some astrophysics researchers to broach the possibility of "timelines" outside of "time" all being simultaneous. That's not something we can practically experience from our normal perspectives. However, the concept of all time being simultaneous outside the zone of our limited perception is a basic metaphysical principle which has been referenced by mystics throughout the ages.

## Mass and Energy

A second conclusion from Einstein's equation is no less powerful than the first, and it states that mass and energy are directly related. To put it another way, mass is simply energy slowed down and "coagulated" into a material form. So everything we experience (or understand to exist) actually exists on a spectrum of energy.

During a lecture by a Stanford University astrophysicist, I finally understood this relationship as he described how mass transfers itself back to energy. For example, if you take a pile of wood and burn it, you get a certain amount of energy released as heat with the residual remaining as ash (mass). If you take an atom from the remaining ash and split it, you have reduced the particle to about as small as we can measure while simultaneously creating a nuclear explosion. That means we can turn almost the entirety of this mass back into energy.

Author Jane Roberts summed up this metaphysical point of view with two quotes in her book, *Dreams, "Evolution," and Value Fulfillment (Volume 1)*:

*"All energy contains consciousness... A recognition of that simple statement would indeed change your world."*[2]

*"Scientists now say that energy and matter are one. They must take the next full step to realize that consciousness and energy and matter are one."*[3]

The bottom line is that human beings are simply energy in the form of mass. But it is, as they say, all a matter of perspective.

- Metaphysics states that divine consciousness has created (and still continues creating) this energy, which then creates mass.
- Science says that everything can be explained (except for human consciousness) if you give us just one miracle (i.e., the "big bang" or "little bang" theory of creation's beginning).
- Most religions say that there is a divine source to things, which at least gives the human "ego" hope for some type of existence after death of the body.

## Inspiration

I believe metaphysics is much more than just a theoretical construct. It may be the closest approximation we can have of what reality is, how it works, and what it means. More importantly, it posits a purely spiritual basis for everything we know and consider to be real.

From my experience, searching for our individual spiritual path is expressing an optimism about our personal worth and power. It's important to recognize that intense and consistent impulses of a positive nature should be pursued. Those will lead to patterns of behavior that will ultimately serve us best.

Early on as an adult, I was influenced by the works and conclusions of the famous analytic psychologist Carl Jung, who believed that organized religion often hinders true spiritual exploration and stifles direct experiences with the Divine.[4] That rang true for me. I began my life within a traditional religious framework, but I felt less and less a part of its doctrine and norms as I matured. Jung's arguments underscore the idea that each individual's spiritual journey is personal and resembles a pilgrimage.

This book hopes to illuminate the viability of a more individual, spiritual exploration beyond traditional frameworks. All of this brings to my mind a saying by the Spanish poet Manuel Machado:

*"Caminante no hay camino. Pero se hace el camino al andar."*

The translation is: "Traveler, there is no trail. But you can make a trail by walking."

For me, this quote means that the quest to strengthen the spiritual leg of our three-legged stool may not be on a well-defined path. Instead, we might be required to blaze our own individual trail, which sometimes involves venturing into areas that fall outside the safe boundaries of our previous personal paradigms.

I hope this discussion will provide you with encouragement and insight that can support you on your spiritual journey.

## Reflections

On a personal note, as I began to contemplate and incorporate the principles of metaphysics, I arrived at a major breakthrough in my beliefs. Specifically, I realized that, prior to this development, I had actually been mad at God.

My childhood view of God had been badly shaken by my early experiences. I didn't want to face my own conclusions that somehow God or organized religion had let humanity down, so I considered myself to be an agnostic or atheist. The feelings of guilt I had been carrying around were essentially suffocating any real thought on the subject.

Through metaphysics, I began looking at myself (and everyone else) as being aspects of a divine source. We each have a physical learning experience for our own reasons. Changing this perspective allowed me to shift from a generalized feeling of guilt to sincere remorse for some of my actions.

Though this may seem like a small change, guilt is truly a crippling emotion and leads to no good end. Replacing that with genuine remorse was life changing—in terms of trauma recovery and a spiritual search. If I had known then what I know now, I would hope to act differently in certain situations.

This new feeling was reinforced by a new outlook. We may all be less-than-proud of particular thoughts and behaviors, but that's no reason to bury ourselves in guilt for the actions in our past.

***<u>Notes:</u>***

1. Roberts, Jane, *Dreams, "Evolution," and Value Fulfillment*, Prentice Hall Press, New York, 1986, p. 345.
2. Roberts, Jane, *Dreams, "Evolution," and Value Fulfillment (Volume 1)*, Prentice Hall, 1979, p. 100.
3. Roberts, Jane, *The Nature of the Psyche: Its Human Expression*, Amber-Allen, 1995. This material and the following paragraphs are largely paraphrased from this book.
4. Jung, Carl, *Memories, Dreams and Reflections*, Vintage, 1989.

Plebe Year at USNA. The good-looking guy on the left was my roommate (later a combat Marine and life-long friend). We are on our way to the Army-Navy game in Philadelphia.

Sports remained my main passion and support throughout my years at the Academy. I always wanted to play, not watch.

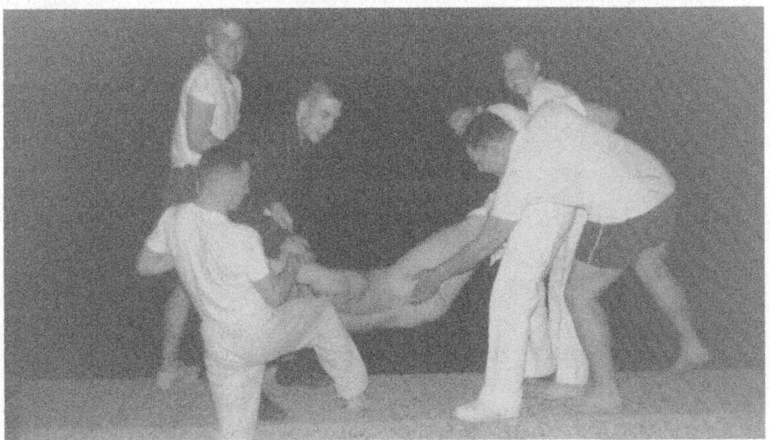

Plebes just following orders, with an upperclassman about to get his "swim quals" in the Academy Reflection Pool.

Brigade Boxing Champs! Boxing classes were mandatory for every Midshipman. Those who liked boxing could follow up on one of the six battalion boxing teams. Following that there were the Brigade Championships to determine Academy winners in each weight class.

Graduation, 1966, from USNA, referred to as "a great place to be from but a hell of a place to be at." Ready to begin "living large" on my $110 per month Ensign's pay.

BUD/S Training. This photo was taken on our last day of BUD/S training in Puerto Rico. The only school left before graduation was Scuba School in Key West, Florida. We skewed the normal graduation numbers by starting with 13 officers and graduating 13 officers, plus 2 Greek Special Forces Officers. Anyone left in the class at this point could run or swim all day.

Army Parachuting School, Ft. Benning, Georgia. A three-week basic course which all SEALs then followed up with skydiving parachute training, called High Altitude Low Opening (HALO) parachuting.

Viet Nam, 1969. Most extractions for my squad were by boat. When in trouble, SEALs always try to head to water.

Like most hunters, we were proud of the results of our efforts that night.

My good friend, Ranger School partner, and fellow SEAL. John "Bubba" Brewton. In 1970, Bubba was shot 6 times on a combat patrol in Viet Nam and subsequently died from his wounds. Bubba loved both Joan Baez and Ayn Rand. His plan was to leave the Navy, marry his fiancée, and return to Alabama.

Me in 1970, feeling older than my years.

Philippines. Not all work occurred above the surface.

Most underwater clandestine operations begin and end on a submarine.

Coronado, California. Ever being volunteered, we were testing a new anti-shark weapon for use by downed aviators. We had two surgeons aboard a Navy experimental ship to handle any mistakes on our part, with a glass bubble underneath for photos. "Chumming" for sharks brought them in herds. Our work was done back-to-back while underwater.

Spain. 1972 to 1975.
As an Olmsted Scholar. "The fish were jumping and the cotton was high." Since often the university students were on strike, or the professors were on strike, or the government had the university closed because of strikes, I visited all parts of Spain in my free time.

Me. Back to work 1976.

Heather begins her "lifetime work in progress" with me.

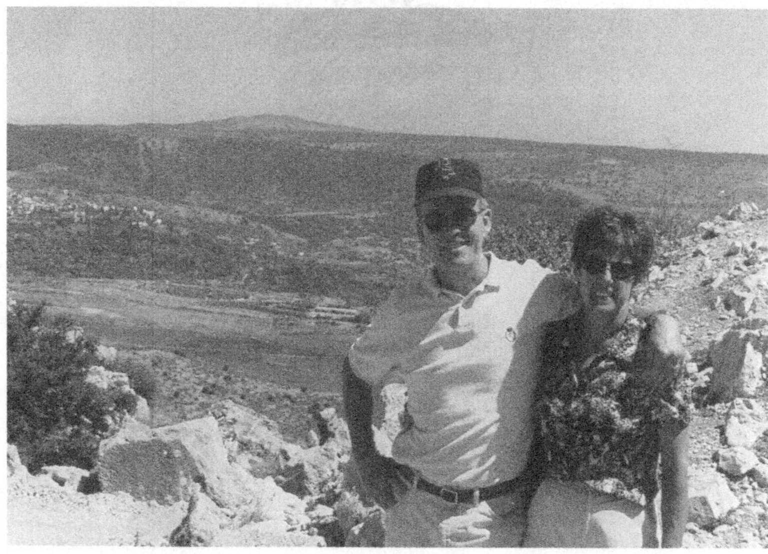

Israel. 1999. When I first married Heather, I thought of her as a diamond in the rough. I hadn't really thought through how rugged diamonds are. I was the one whose edges needed sanding.

# CHAPTER 13
# CHANNELING

*"Ultimately, your greatest teacher is to live with an open heart."*
**—Pat Rodegast/Emmanuel**

I wasn't initially sure what to think about the concept of channeling, but then I was truly intrigued by what I learned as I personally began to explore this phenomenon. And the more knowledgeable I became, the more discerning I became and the more I wanted to know. Somehow, many normal people were tapping into extraordinary wisdom from another time or place and sharing it for the benefit of others.

The truth is, we are all channels. We are constantly receiving impulses and hunches that come from beyond what we call our intellects. If we just desire to listen, we can be open to hear our own hearts. Some individuals seem more open to this than others, and many creative people throughout history have credited this ability for their creative arts.

I realize some people may be uncomfortable with a subject like this because they don't have any direct experience with it. That's natural, but it can also lead to dismissing an idea before they have any real knowledge about it. At this point, if this is brand new to you, I would just ask that you allow me to discuss this subject while you keep an open mind.

After more than forty years of research in this field, I can state that the underlying messages of reputable channeled sources all point in the same direction with regard to basic spiritual principles. Their tone and style can vary dramatically, but there's a consistency in their intent to be extremely loving and supportive.

It's difficult to overemphasize the positive impact that the information received by the channels I will discuss has had on my life. Because of that, this chapter is devoted to highlighting just a few of the humans who have generously brought us consequential knowledge from somewhere beyond the world as we know it.

## Definitions

Channeling has been around for as long as recorded history. Examples abound in the Bible's Old Testament and New Testament within the Christian religion, along with truly ancient accounts in almost every other major religious tradition on earth. For a specific instance, simply recall the biblical tale of God delivering the Ten Commandments to Moses.

The word "channeling" is used now extensively in metaphysical discussions to describe a certain type of activity involving a person ("the channel") and information which comes through the channel from a non-personal source.

A person who channels may be fully conscious, be partially conscious, or be fully unconscious while receiving messages. This latter form of channeling is normally referred to as "full trance channeling" or simply "trance channeling."

Someone who channels can be thought of as a kind of telephone through which messages pass. The channel should not be confused with the message. The channel simply acts as a conduit though which information is transmitted.

I'd also like to point out that channels are nothing other than ordinary people and certainly not "saints," per se. And neither the channel nor the message should be accepted without passing the information through both our intellect and our intuition to see if it rings true for us personally and seems useful. My goal with these examples is to broaden an understanding of the metaphysical principles they espouse, along with other sources and teachings. I hope to highlight the breadth, scope, and quality of their works, as well as the works of others.

For simplicity, I'll use the male pronoun "he" to refer to the non-physical metaphysical teachers who have shared messages through these channels. However, all of these teachers state that the totality of their beings encompasses both male and female aspects, as well as aspects that are neither.

### *Jane Roberts*

American author Jane Roberts produced more than 20 books providing a view of what she experienced when channeling. The teacher who delivered the messages through Roberts described himself as a non-physical entity whom they called Seth.

Twelve of these books can properly be called "Seth books," since Seth dictated them though Roberts while she was in a full trance. Videotapes that captured some of this process demonstrate that Seth's voice and mannerisms do not resemble Jane's at all.

Jane's husband, Robert Butts, acted as a scribe throughout the dictation of these books, and Seth's delivery was often so rapid that Rob could hardly keep up. The material available from Seth seemed inexhaustible on any topic they would choose, which caused Jane at one point to jokingly say to Rob, "I wish Seth could also type."

Jane Roberts truly was one of the most prolific mystics of our age and, early in this endeavor, she describes these experiences in her book, *The God of Jane*:

*"Since later 1963, I've clocked approximately 4,000 hours of trance time, during which the Seth sessions have been held twice weekly... My trance time is more concentrated than regular time. I'm not unconscious but conscious in a different way, at another level... This state of perception has nothing to do with classical pathological dissociation; and its products—Seth's five books—display a highly developed intellect at work and give evidence of a special kind of creativity.*

*"In those trance hours, I 'turn into' someone else. At least I am not myself to myself; I become Seth, or a part of what Seth is. I don't feel 'possessed' or 'invaded' during sessions. I don't feel that some super spirit has 'taken over' my body. Instead, it's as if I'm practicing some precise psychological art, one that is ancient and poorly understood in our culture; or as if I'm learning a psychological science that helps me map the contours of consciousness itself...*

*After all this time, I'm finally examining the trance view of reality and comparing it to the official views of science and religion."*[1]

Seth describes himself as a teacher and, more specifically, as a "personality essence no longer focused in physical reality." That simple description is woefully inadequate in describing the demeanor, knowledge, and characteristics of the entity known as Seth to Jane and Rob, and subsequently to students and readers in many countries.

In the preamble to his first book, *Seth Speaks: The Eternal Validity of the Soul*, Seth says:

*"If you believe firmly that your consciousness is locked up somewhere inside your skull and is powerless to escape it, if you feel that your consciousness ends at the boundary of your body, then you sell yourself short, and you will think that I am a delusion. I am no more a delusion than you are.*

*"I can say this to each of my readers honestly: I am older than you are, and at least in terms of age as you think of it. If a writer can qualify as any kind of authority on the basis of age, therefore, then I should get a medal. I am an energy personality essence, no longer focused in physical matter. As such, I am aware of some truths that many of you seem to have forgotten. I hope to remind you of these."*[2]

In this book, Seth describes his reality (and our human reality) from his perspective, and he generally outlines the material he plans to dictate through Jane and Rob over the next years, with their cooperation.

What first struck me about this material was that Seth orally dictated the content of a book to Rob, while Jane was in a trance and Seth was fully in charge of her body and speech. This wasn't some kind of rambling extemporaneous monologue. Seth rarely corrected a word in a sentence. He spelled out any words which might be misunderstood, and he even provided grammatical directions regarding emphasis, underlining, and use of capital letters.

Having recently just finished writing a Ph.D. dissertation, with all my stumbles and rewrites and multiple full edits, I was in awe of this truly superhuman capability to verbally dictate final, meaningful copy without mistakes.

The other thing that struck me was that each of Seth's sentences was perfectly clear, and the logical flow between sentences, paragraphs, and full chapters was impeccable. I was completely amazed before I even slowed down to assess the full import of what Seth was actually saying.

Stop for a second and think about the pure scope of this feat.

Twelve books, all exploring aspects of our human condition, were orally dictated by Seth through Jane Roberts in a full trance, without any errors not caused by a misunderstanding on the part of Jane or her husband Rob (as scribe). By itself, this is nothing less than an incredible demonstration of unrivaled skill.

The first two books of the Seth series *(Seth Speaks: The Eternal Validity of the Soul* and *The Nature of Personal Reality)* quite literally changed my perception of my life. I felt like a "light bulb" turned on inside of me when I recognized the incredibly supportive structure of learning in these volumes of work. I am a person who wants a logical progression of knowledge when learning any subject (going from "a" to "b," then from "b" to "c," then "c" to "d," and so on). The Seth books do this in an exemplary fashion if read in the order they were produced.

Before she died, Jane also produced a series of different books. These were completed without Seth, but they were largely produced while in trance or referencing her trance activities. What they had in common with her earlier works is that they were all extraordinary in depth, scope, and content.

The published works and the voluminous notes and background materials of Jane Roberts and Robert Butts are now available through Yale University for research purposes. I believe that no one can read these books without experiencing a greatly enhanced and life-supporting belief structure about what it means to be a human being.

After I finished the series of Seth books, I began widely reading the works of other metaphysical authors over the years. As mentioned, what I have found is a great similarity in perspective among them, but with a hugely varying manner of producing their materials.

This gave me an even greater appreciation for Seth. His books were sequentially clear, while other materials often took some of the underlying fundamentals for granted. That was like trying to understand a third-year chemistry book without having read and understood the first two years' texts.

### *Alice A. Bailey*

Another extremely influential channel was Alice A. Bailey, who made her first channeled contact by telepathy with a Tibetan monk in 1919 while she was praying in church. Without ever meeting the monk, whom she referred to as The Tibetan, they began thirty years of work via channeled contact, which resulted in over twenty books of metaphysical materials.

In her autobiography, titled *Unfinished Autobiography* and published in 1951, Bailey describes her first contact with The Tibetan and her life and work from that point forward. She died within thirty days of completing the last of the work she agreed to channel for The Tibetan.[3]

In the books, The Tibetan describes himself as a Tibetan disciple of a certain degree, living on the border of Tibet, and in charge of a group of other Tibetan monks. Here's an example:

> *"...(I am) a brother of yours, who has travelled a little longer upon the Path than has the average student, and has therefore incurred greater responsibilities. I am one who has wrestled and fought his way into a greater measure of light than has the aspirant who will read this article, and I must act as a transmitter of the light, no matter what the cost."*

The Tibetan further admonishes against blind obedience to any teacher or saint, and states:

> *"If the teaching conveyed calls forth a response from the illumined mind of the worker in the world, and brings a flashing forth of his intuition, then let that teaching be accepted. But not otherwise."*[4]

### *Jach Pursel*

Known as a full-trance channel, Jach Pursel is a Florida man who shares messages from an entity who refers to himself as Lazarus. The Lazaris material, as it's called, has been delivered through

Jach Pursel for many years, and it is available online or in the form of video and audio tapes, books, and CDs.

The scope and depth of this material speaks for itself, and the phenomenon of listening to Lazarus is always enlightening and entertaining. I personally believe that a sure sign of a master teacher is a source who has a fine sense of humor along with delivering meaningful messages.

Through Pursel, we learned that Lazarus gave assurances that he and the others haven't come to save our planet. We're capable of doing that ourselves, he indicates, if we will only remember our power and ability to do so. Their mission is to remind us of our powers.

The second purpose of his messages is to stress that we create our own reality—through love, choice, and the power to change. The third reason is to remind us to find out how completely and profoundly we're loved, and what profound powers of love we have ourselves. Finally, he prompts us to dream, to remember our dreams, and to value them, as a creative power.[5]

### *Esther Hicks*

Another full-trance channel is named Esther Hicks. She currently resides in Boerne, Texas, and has a worldwide following. Along with her husband Jerry Hicks, Esther began with a broad interest in metaphysics and meditation practices before evolving into a truly remarkable channel for an entity referred to as Abraham.[6] I will discuss the work of this remarkable channel in more detail as we proceed in this book.

Again, Esther and Abraham materials are available in almost all media formats, and the messages align with Seth, Lazarus, and other major channeled sources.

### *Meredith Young-Sowers*

Living in Walpole, New Hampshire, in 1981, Meredith Lady Young-Sowers is a woman who began receiving messages through channeled, automatic writing from a teacher she calls Mentor. In her book, *Agartha*, first published in 1983, she described the sequence of events around this phenomenon in her life and the necessary mental and emotional adjustments which resulted from it.

Mentor purports to be a non-physical metaphysical teacher, and his communications are extremely direct and succinct on many issues affecting our human situation. As with almost all other non-physical teachers, Mentor states that names are of no importance, so he made some simple recommendations and Young chose to call him "Mentor."

Mentor's teachings begin with a statement that there is no rush for us to see beyond our present moments as we open our minds to the gifts of increasing awareness. Beginning each day with a time of quiet and a clearing and deepening of awareness of our mind is the starting point. As a search for our personal truth begins by opening ourselves to new experiences and learning, we can push forward on our individual paths in trust and optimism.

A central theme of Mentor's teaching is the importance of love. His definition goes beyond what we might normally think of this term:

> *"Love is experienced by all dimensions as it fits the needs of those involved. Thus, you could call my love 'abstract love' and your love 'emotional release love' (love that is dominated by individual priorities). Connecting these two realms is 'enlightened love,' which is love through enlightenment or total awareness. Enlightenment is the traveling, the traveler, and the point to which one travels. It*

*is the doorway and the experience of triangulating on love beyond the physical. Love actually knows no boundaries and, through enlightenment, can open vastly divergent panoramas from those to which you have become accustomed.*[7]

*"The insights of the heart and the perceptions of worlds beyond exist equally for us all. They are not learned. They simply are. And metaphysics is based on the proposition that this expanded awareness is available to all who seek it.*[8]

In summary, Mentor tells us that each individual's belief structure is largely responsible for how he or she views the world, and that will determine whether or not our minds can or will open to the type of input data which the spiritual portion of ourselves can provide.

***

As the famous TV sports announcer Howard Cosell used to say, "And the list goes on and on."

I always found it interesting to see the close personal bonds channels develop with these spiritual teachers. They often spend hours in conversation across many years. But perhaps the most surprising thing about channelers and channeling is the enormous breadth and scope of so many independent channels and sources of these materials.

The quality and import of some channeled materials are simply undeniable but, as with any subject worthy of human attention and research, it's incumbent upon us to use our innate sense of best judgment in assessing new ideas and concepts.

***Notes:***

1. Roberts, Jane, *The God of Jane, A Psychic Manifesto*, Prentiss-Hall, New Jersey, 1981, pp. 3-4. Along with her 20 books, Jane Roberts and her husband Rob transferred thousands of pages of both public and private Seth sessions, personal journals, written records and notes, Seth tapes, and photos to Yale University Library for researchers and public use.
2. Roberts, Jane, *Seth Speaks: The Eternal Validity of the Soul*, Amber-Allen and New World Publishing, 1994, Preamble page.
3. Bailey, Alice A., *Unfinished Autobiography*, Lucis Publishing, 1994.
4. Bailey, Alice A., *A Treatise on Cosmic Fire*, Lucis Publishing, 1925, pp. ix-x.
5. Reed, Henry, and Cayce, Charles Thomas, edited, *Edgar Cayce on Channeling Your Higher Self*, p. 8.
6. For an excellent starting book, see the teachings of Abraham in, Hicks, Esther and Jerry, *Ask and It Is Given*, Hay House, Carlsbad, California, 2004.
7. Young, *Agartha,* ibid., pp. 70-71.
8. *Agartha,* ibid., p. 90.

# CHAPTER 14
# FACETS OF METAPHYSICS

*"Consciousness creates form. It is not the other way around."*
**—Jane Roberts/Seth**

While the reasoning mind has led to science and all of its achievements, it is not the only "tool" available to help us explore reality. Metaphysics encourages us to stretch our boundaries, as you saw with channeling in the last chapter. Additional innate tools can also play an important role in our spiritual journeys, and this chapter will feature some of those and the underlying structures.

## Consciousness

The human body is comprised of 59 elements. Six of those elements (carbon, oxygen, hydrogen, nitrogen, calcium, and phosphorus) constitute over 99% of what makes a human being. What is more interesting is that all of these elements are inert.[1]

So where does human consciousness come from?

Science, with all of its advances, cannot make a single living cell of consciousness from any combination of inert materials, much less replicate the functioning of the human mind. Taking that into account, we have to conclude that having our consciousness with the ability to think and reason is a *miracle*. Even though science says we are simply a legacy of our DNA and evolutionary development, that leaves so very much unexplained in terms of understanding the basic miracle of life and our human role in it.

Let's look at the origin.

As human beings, our first experience with life as babies is becoming aware of our personal consciousness. We use that consciousness to begin assessing our perceptions of the world around us. This involves using our physical senses to interpret everything we encounter.

But we also come equipped with personal "internal sensors" that are provided by the greater portions of our psyche or total consciousness, which are aware of their own capabilities. These allow us to intuitively know that all our experiences somehow matter and that we can utilize these "non-awake" portions of our being to assist us in making judgments about what we experience.

So, for anyone truly desiring to understand themselves as humans and to explore the meaning of life, it's important to continue to call upon all of our faculties, not just our reasoning ego mind.

The truth is, our conscious reality doesn't need anyone's belief to be what it is. The spiritual teacher Seth describes aspects of energy, consciousness, and the psyche far better than I can.

*"In certain terms, science and religion are both dealing with the idea of an objectively created universe. Either God 'made it,' or physical matter, in some unexplained manner, was formed after an initial explosion of energy, and consciousness emerged from the initially dead matter in a way yet to be explained. Instead, consciousness formed matter…. Consciousness and matter and energy are one, but consciousness initiates the transformation of energy into matter."*[2]

And to continue:

*"Now if you are looking for a simple definition to explain the psyche, I will be of no help. If you want to experience the splendid creativity of your own being, however, then I will use methods that will arouse your greatest adventuresomeness, your boldest faith in yourself, and I will paint pictures of your psyche that will lead you to experience even its broadest reaches, if you so desire. The psyche, then, is not a known land. It is not simply an alien land, to which or through which you can travel. It is not completed or nearly complete subjective universe there for you to explore. It is, instead, an ever-forming state of being, in which your present sense of existence resides. You create it and it creates you."*[3]

This reminds me of a wonderful quote that applies for anyone who believes that life has no meaning beyond what science can prove with its instruments and techniques:

*"A leaf doesn't need to believe in photosynthesis to turn green."*

In other words, if the meaning of life involves a divine source and an afterlife, those things will exist whether we believe in them or not.

What we ultimately find is that consciousness is much bigger and broader in scope than we might initially think. There's much more to it.

As we utilize and strengthen our reasoning, other innate consciousness capabilities can be experienced and examined. Some of these include precognitive dreams, astral travel, telepathy, clairvoyance, out-of-body experiences and, of course, channeling. These expanded forms of consciousness have been experienced and recorded by humans of all kinds and at every age.

## Reincarnation

While I was still at the Naval Academy, I read my first book written by the British-born American novelist Taylor Caldwell, who was born in 1900 and died in 1985.

During her very interesting life, Caldwell wrote and published more than 50 novels, and she kept manuscripts of 140+ other books that were unpublished. Her novels often focused on historical figures or eras, ranging from antiquity to modern times. Samples of her novels include *Dear and Glorious Physician* (about St. Luke), *Ceremony of the Innocent* (about Cicero), and *The Earth is the Lord's* (about the life of Genghis Kahn).

Later, I came across a biography about Caldwell that was written by well-known author Jess Stern. Their connection was fascinating.

Stern initially met Caldwell when they were seated next to each other at a writer's dinner in Los Angeles. At the time, Caldwell was 70 years old and recently divorced. She was suffering from severe depression and felt that her writing career was over.

During their discussions that evening, Stern suggested Caldwell might try age-regression hypnosis to help her recover from her recent trauma. Caldwell was initially reluctant but ultimately agreed.

Two medically qualified hypnotists in the Los Angeles area agreed to treat Caldwell, and the sessions were recorded on tape. As it turned out, Caldwell was an excellent, fully somnambulant, hypnotic subject. The tapes of these sessions became the genesis of the biography that Stern wrote about Caldwell.

Under hypnosis, Caldwell was regressed to her birth and early years, and she had complete recall of many events. This, in itself, was unusual but not unheard of.

In subsequent sessions, Caldwell was regressed to before her birth as Taylor Caldwell and provided complete recollections of lifetimes lived in the eras of her novels. Her personages in these prior eras were not the subjects of her novels, but were simply humans living in each of these time frames. When Caldwell listened to the tapes, she was astounded to hear what had emerged during the hypnosis sessions.

Metaphysics postulates that our consciousness isn't limited by the physical expiration of our human bodies. Past lives and future lives are part of who we are, whether we access that information or not.

Providing his take on reincarnation, the French philosopher Voltaire addressed those who believe that we only live once and then go to heaven or hell:

> *"...It is no more a miracle to be born twice than it is to be born once."*

This is an extremely interesting thought to contemplate.

The fact that the energy source we call our souls will often choose to live more than one human lifetime is a given in all metaphysical texts. To put death into perspective, Esther Hicks/Abraham refers to dying as "croaking," not to be feared as an end, but rather looked at as a simple transition.

Another teacher, Pat Rodegast/Emmanuel, describes the sensation of dying as akin to taking off an old pair of shoes, loved but worn-out and pinching, and then running free through the grass barefoot like a little child.

One of my favorite teachers was a Lebanese-American writer named Kahlil Gibran. His book, *The Prophet,* has reportedly sold more copies than any other book but the Bible, and it has been my constant companion for the past forty or so years. It is an incredible little book with a huge message, and this quote reinforces the principle of reincarnation:

*"A little while, a moment of rest upon the wind, and another woman shall bear me.*[5]

## Spiritual Guides

In Taylor Caldwell's last two hypnosis sessions, a "Guide" appeared and spoke through her and described his role in helping Caldwell write all of her novels. Caldwell later reported that she had never been aware of this "Guide" or of his assistance. However, she admitted that she rarely did any deep research while producing any of her books. The words of the text just seemed to flow out naturally.

That was remarkable, considering the extraordinary depth of detail she included in her novels about bygone eras and her understanding of the characters' mindsets at that time.

The "Guide" also stated that Caldwell would get married again and continue to write. She found this highly unlikely at her age, but the prophecy was accurate. Not long after this time, she met and married a third husband and published an additional seven novels (including *I Judas*, about the life of Judas Iscariot) before her death in 1980.

We have overwhelming evidence that humans have lived prior lives, and we can make an excellent case for proving that our consciousness continues after death. For example, consider the many accounts of near-death experiences shared by individuals who have been resuscitated or otherwise brought back to consciousness from a near-death state. These people consistently report experiencing the continuation of full cognitive consciousness following physical unconsciousness.

If you are interested, I recommend reading *Reincarnation for the Millions*, a straight-forward yet very readable overview of reincarnation doctrines, historically and culturally, by author Susy Smith.

## Intuition

In 2004, Heather and I were in our home in Austin, Texas. One night, I experienced an OOBE in which someone knocked at the front door. When I opened it, I did not recognize the young man standing there. But as soon as he began to speak, I realized that it was my dad from many years earlier.

Waves of his love swept over me, and I invited him inside. He said he didn't have time to stay, but he stepped in for a moment and then left. Afterwards, I recorded the event in a journal and then described it to Heather while we were headed to the airport very early the next morning for a skiing trip.

After dropping off our bags and skis at the counter, I decided to check my phone for any messages. That's when I heard the voice of my sister's son Joe saying that my 93-year-old father had died peacefully during the night.

Science can't explain that, but it was unequivocally real to me.

This is just another reminder that the reasoning mind isn't the only "tool" available to us in a spiritual search. We can tap into richer experiences by leveraging other parts of our consciousness like intuition and instincts. And we should never discard actual human experiences of things beyond explanation by science or religion, simply because they say it isn't possible or correct according to current paradigms or dogmas.

Jane Roberts/Seth gives very good advice on this subject:

> *"You should never accept as fact a theory that contradicts your own experience. Man's experience includes, for example, all kinds of behavior for which science has no answers. Science cannot be blamed for saying that its methods are not conducive to the study of this or that area of experience—but science should at least be rapped on the knuckles smartly if it automatically rejects such behavior as valid, legitimate, or real, or when it attempts to place such events outside the realm of actuality. Science can justly be reprimanded when it tries to pretend that man's experience is limited to those events that science can explain."*[6]

Metaphysics gives us the tools to think about our lives as a more fluid existence with greater possibilities. When the ego's understanding and awareness expands to encompass the fact that we are all eternal souls having human experiences, it loses its fear of death. And the release of that fear of death brings great relief to the ego portion of our being.

***Notes:***

1. Bryson, Bill, *The Body: A Guide for Occupants*, Random House, New York, 2019. This is a fascinating book with lots of interesting facts.
2. Roberts, Jane, *Dreams, "Evolution," and Value Fulfillment (Volume I),* Prentiss Hall, New York, pp. 120-121.
3. Roberts, Jane, *Psyche*, op. cit., p. 12.
4. Stern, Jess, *The Search for a Soul: Taylor Caldwell's Psychic Lives,* Fawcett Crest Books, 1974.
5. Gibran, Khalil, *The Prophet*, Fingerprint Publishing, 2018, p. 96.
6. Roberts, Jane, *Dreams, "Evolution," and Value Fulfillment (Volume II),* Amber-Allen, 1997, p 497. In addition to her 20 novels, Jane Roberts had well over 1,000 sessions with Seth which were recorded. The first 510 sessions were subsequently published in book form, with a total of 9 additional volumes.

# CHAPTER 15
# "GOD"

*"…(I believe) that God isn't a being, but a state of being… and I was now in that state of being. In other words, that enlightenment isn't meeting God; it is a state of clearly knowing oneself as part of God/Goddess/All That Is."*[1]

**—Anita Moorjani**

*"Each person alive is part of the living God, supported in life by the magnificent power of nature, which is God translated into the elements of earth and the universe."*[2]

**— Jane Roberts/Seth**

As I have discussed in earlier chapters, my personal view of God or Source has changed dramatically over the years. This chapter is designed to broaden positively the whole conversation.

Discussions about the origins of our lives inevitably begin with the fundamental idea that there is a divine creator—or there isn't. Since one purpose of this book is to challenge you to open your mind to the broadest possible concept of a divine source for everything, I won't linger on the scientific point of view. This states that an unexplained initial event or accident and subsequent mindless evolution account for our current situation.

We likely can't overestimate how the various concepts of "God" and "God's messages" have affected humanity throughout our recorded history (and, I suspect, way before that). Humans have used their intellects to believe in one God, to believe in multiple Gods, or to believe there is no divine source by any name and that everything is an unexplainable accident.

The concept or word "God" has historically meant vastly different things to differing groups of humans. For some people, God is either "up there" or "out there" somewhere. Some say he judges us, while others believe he doesn't judge anything he has created. Still others may think he favors certain groups of humans.

Christians believe that the Deity is three in one: The Father, The Son, and The Holy Spirit. Hindus believe in multiple gods and goddesses. Buddhists believe in a divine source that is not describable in human terms of he or she or by any other words.

The "rules" of these groups vary. Christians have to accept baptism and the concept of a three-in-one Deity if they want to go to heaven. Some Christians now feel that they must be "born again" and accept Jesus Christ as a personal savior in addition to baptism. The Catholic Church mandates that people can't enter heaven without a Christian baptism, no matter how good or blameless their lives have been.

The same ambiguity applies to "God's word." Compare the Christian Bible, the Islamic Quran, the Jewish Torah, and the

Book of Mormon. Which version is correct? It's worth noting that crusades, wars, and genetic "cleansings" are continually justified by participants claiming that God is one their side—and not on the other side. For example, during World War II, many Germans wore belt buckles etched with the phrase, "Gott mit uns," meaning "God is on our side."

## The Metaphysical Point of View

The metaphysical viewpoint, which aligns with the view of "mystics" of all ages, is that there is a divine source to our situation. However, this It/He/She/One Source is essentially not fully describable at the level of human consciousness.

The term "God" is articulated by many metaphysical sources as "All That Is," and I see these terms as synonymous. To me, the difference is that the term "All That Is" doesn't carry the baggage that the term "God" can engender. With that said, our vision of "God" (or "All That Is") is crucial to our mental and emotional stance as individual human beings in this world. It colors almost every other thought that comes into our minds.

No short, excerpted descriptions of the divine source of which we all are a part can do any justice to the direct experience of this divinity (called a "mystical" experience by some). Admittedly, a variety of books have made valiant efforts to capture the depth and beauty of Deity. My goal here is simply to use quotes from several metaphysical teachers that try to evoke the feelings of something that is truly indescribable.

> *"It is very difficult to try to assign anything like human motivation to All That Is. I can only say that it is possessed by 'the need' to lovingly create from its own being; to lovingly transform its own reality in such a way that each most slight probable consciousness*

*can come to be (long pause); and with the need to see that any and all possible orchestrations of consciousness have the chance to emerge, to perceive and to love."*[3]

—Jane Roberts/Seth

*"This concept may raise the question whether God is personal or impersonal, directing intelligence or law and principle. Human beings, since they experience life with a dualistic consciousness, tend to believe that either the one or the other is true. Yet God is both. But God's personal aspect does not mean personality. God is not a person residing in a certain place, though it is possible to have a personal God-experience within the self.*

*For the only place God can be looked for and found is within, not in any other place. God's existence can be deduced outside the self from the beauty of creation, from the manifestations of nature, from the wisdom collected by philosophers and scientists. But such observations become an experience of God only when God's presence is felt first within. The inner experience of God is the greatest of all experiences because it contains all desirable experiences."*[4]

—Rochelle Diane Sparrow

*"The Godsource has always loved you. The thought, which is the Godsource expressed, has never judged one of you. Man created judgment through religion and dogma to keep you in line. But the Godsource, the All That Is, the All in All, has never judged you for any one thing. He has allowed you—through love—to exist, to dance around on the stage of this illusionary adventure called the human drama."*[5]

—J.Z. Knight/Ramptha

*"God is the composite of all life-force energy, both the celestial forces and the internal forces of one's heart. God is the total living force of the universe. Therefore, when one prays to God, one is praying to a whole, with varying aspects of the working whole influencing every solution. Therefore God, the Isness, the Great Oneness of the Universe, is the collective presence of all things living, all evolving beings."*[6]

—Meredith Young-Sowers/Mentor

*"Thus, man is indeed God. His eventual path is always toward awareness of his own divinity, is always toward consciousness of his Godly nature... There is no God waiting to reward you or judge you; there is only self coming to terms with self and realizing your own God essence."*[7]

—Saemmi Muth/Vywamus

I'd like to add one additional quote, which is an excerpt from a trance channel named Judith Coates, who brings forward messages from an entity identified as Jeshua ben Joseph:

*"We have spoken often of the holy child's adventure, of how you have thought so wondrously to focus on a specific experience and expression known as a lifetime, a personality, and individuality.*

*"You say, 'This is who I am. I am this individuality. I go by a certain name. I have certain qualities and attributes. I have certain employment and relationships that define me. This is who I am.' You forget that you are a most wondrous being, that you can call for a specific focus to the near exclusion of remembrance.*

*"As the holy child in divine creativity, you set a thread of remembrance and connection to your total self. This still, small voice within says, 'Yes, you are this, but you are more. Come home. Remember.' It is as if you set a certain time on your alarm clock to receive an insistent call to awaken. That is what you are responding to in this lifetime.*

*"It is a call to awaken to the totality of Self. It is not that you forget or deny your individuality. It is not to say that this dimension, this reality, is all bad, that it is just an illusion, that it has been a mistake. You chose to experience this reality and all that you scripted into this dimension.*

*"The still, small voice calls to awaken you now to the totality to remember the Christ of you and to commit to the discipleship to that Christ. We do not speak here of Jeshua ben Joseph, of Jesus, but to the Christ of you, the Christ of the <u>One</u>.*

*"In Truth, the Christ is not a 'who.' The Christ is your divinity. The Christ is the essence of your totality. We have likened it to a vast ocean out of which you fashioned for yourself a drop of water as an experience, and you said, 'I am the drop of water. I am separate. I am individual.' Then you saw yourself as separate from the ocean. The Christ of you is the beingness, the isness, the vast ocean of the totality of Self—with a capital S."*[8]

There is much food for thought in the above quotations and, by themselves, they are simply representative of a vast quantity of truly inspirational metaphysical material available on the subject of our divine source.

## The Question of Prayer

How and when to pray (and to whom) is a subject which is central to our perception of ourselves.

When I was little, I was taught that we didn't pray directly to God, but rather to aspects or representatives of God, such as Jesus, Mary, or the Holy Spirit. I always felt that Jesus was probably overwhelmed with other people's prayers, so my favorite was to pray to Mother Mary when I wanted to ask for help with something.

That changed when I got older. I went through the formal Sacrament of Confirmation in the Catholic Church, and I selected Saint Sebastian, The Patron Saint of Athletes and Warriors, as my personal saint and guardian. My step-mother Meemaw chose to pray to Saint Teresa ("The Little Flower") and Saint Jude, the Patron Saint of Lost Causes.

## Active Spirituality

So where does all of this leave us with regard to prayer and the concept of "God"?

All the spiritual teachers I've referenced say, in one way or another, that we all have the same connection to a divine source. Some people consciously open a channel to receive messages from aspects of that source, while others don't.

The important thing to note is that none of these teachers wishes to establish a new religion. None wish to be worshipped. Their attitudes can best be summed up by a phrase in a wonderful book by Mary-Margaret Moore called *I Come as a Brother:* "They are not here to take over. They are simply here to help."

This reminds me of something one of my lifelong friends likes to say: "I'm not just a pretty face; I'm here to help."

From the metaphysical standpoint, we are all aspects of divinity having a human experience. Our interactions with our personal sources can be a conversation or an active prayer for help and support.

The Sufi mystic poet Hafiz refers to God in his poems as "the Friend, Beloved, the Problem Giver and Solver, Sweet Uncle," and many other names for a loved one. This is how I currently feel about the connection. It is both extremely personal, closer to us than our breath, and yet universal. It can and should be talked with and counted on for support, advice (in whatever form it comes), and increased understanding.

Active spirituality involves an ongoing relationship and feeling of connectedness to the divine source, by whatever name resonates with each person. Pick a name that seems appropriate for your Higher Self and open yourself to regular dialogue. When you are asking for help, clarity, or guidance, take time to get still and listen. Then query your intuition.

***Notes:***

1. Moorjani, Anita, *Dying To Be Me*, Hay House, 2002, p. 68. This book relates her personal story of her conscious experience of divinity while being in a full near-death coma.
2. Roberts, Jane, *The Nature of the Psyche: Its Human Expression,* Amber-Allen, 1979, p. 116.
3. Roberts, *Dreams, Vol. 1*, op. cit., p. 129.
4. Sparrow, Diane, *Sedona Journal of Emergence,* May 2003, p. 48.
5. Knight, J.Z., and Mahr, Douglas, *Destination Freedom*, Prentice Hall Press, New York, 1988, p. 50.
6. Young-Sowers, Meredith Lady, *Agartha*, Stillpoint Publishing, 1984, p. 336.

7. Muth, Saemmi, Vywamus and Group, "Embracing Your Christed Resonance," *Sedona Journal of Emergence*, February 1996, pp. 14-15.
8. Coates, Judith. This excerpt was originally from the channeling "Evening with Jeshua" presented in San Diego, California, in 1999, and reproduced in the *Sedona Journal of Emergence,* August 2023, pp. 14-16.

# CHAPTER 16
# ENLIGHTENMENT

*"Before enlightenment, I chopped wood and carried water.*
*After enlightenment, I chopped wood and carried water."*
**—Zen Koan**

*"The real voyage of discovery consists not in seeking new landscapes but in having new eyes."*
**—Marcel Proust**

Before jumping over the fantail to abandon ship at this point, think of the concept of "enlightenment" as a desired direction instead of a destination. We are all on a life path having a certain amount of light, and moving towards a better-lit path should be nothing more than common sense.

## Definition

The word "enlightenment" conjures up the idea of some superhuman accomplishment, but it is simply our natural state of *felt* oneness with being.

*Enlightenment* is the conscious understanding of all that we are as spiritual beings. Humans in this state of awareness have fully accepted both their humanity and their innate divinity. The mental and emotional state that results is known as enlightenment.

## The Path of Enlightenment

Eckhardt Tolle is one of the world's most famous spiritual teachers, and the concept of enlightenment is one of the primary topics he discusses. His books and teachings have been translated into more than forty languages, and his impact is undeniable.

Tolle's personal backstory is truly incredible. He was born in post-World War II Germany and grew up to be largely self-educated. However, he was extremely fearful and paranoid, to the point where he was often afraid to leave his own home. He also suffered from long-term depression.

He was 29 years old and living in London in 1977 when his entire personality changed overnight. Awakening in the morning, he described finding himself completely peaceful and with a feeling that the "self" that he was had completely disappeared.

The effects of this change in his personality were permanent, and the wisdom that began to flow forth made him literally a spiritual teacher and phenomenon, even today. His books, CDs, tapes, and public appearances are both penetrating and powerful, and his approach to spiritual living and enlightenment has impacted the lives of millions.

Tolle makes this important concept and human goal understandable, and he believes it is ultimately attainable for everyone.

*"Once there is a certain degree of Presence, of still and alert attention in human beings' perception, they can sense the divine life essence, the one indwelling consciousness or spirit in every creature, every life-form, recognize it as one with their own essence and so love it as themselves. Until this happens, however, most humans see only the outer forms, unaware of the inner essence, just as they are unaware of their own essence and identify only with their own physical and psychological form."*[1]

To amplify that definition, I'd like to quote another wonderful source of metaphysical spiritual material. Eva Pierrakos channeled an inspired series of books call *The Pathwork Series*, which I feel that every human would benefit by reading.

*"It is the ultimate aim of self-realization to establish the truth of God, of eternal life, of the benign meaning of everything in every crevice of consciousness… This process is the very reason for incarnation and purification…The greatest truth of God's reality and immediacy brings you to the ultimate good that is beyond all question and doubt."*[2]

Spiritual teacher Meredith Young-Sowers further defined enlightenment by reducing it to a more simplified state of human consciousness. For example:

> *"Enlightenment, as a perception, is a clear vision of the perfectness of all things. When this vision fuses with the spiritual body, the result is a kinesthetic reaction of such proportion that there can be no doubt that a foot has been placed upon eternity's threshold."*[3]

The pursuit of enlightenment involves asking some tough questions and, undoubtedly, wrestling with the answers:

- Can we, as humans, actually connect with a "divine presence" within ourselves? What does that feel like?
- We are biased in favor of our ability to use our intellects. Is this really the ultimate achievement for a human?
- Is it possible that our abilities to reason and think are not crowning achievements but merely stepping stones for us as we unfold as humans?
- Can we unfold past the sole use of "reason" in this lifetime?

## The Expansion of Consciousness

Most of the teachers referenced in this book speak of our abilities to experience, individually and personally, a profound transformation of our human consciousness in this lifetime. If the challenge appears enormous, so does the reward.

A way to look at the process of enlightenment and mystical connection is simply an "expansion of consciousness." Our normal consciousness operates within a certain range of vibration, but we can also innately access a broader range of consciousness through focuses such as the practice of meditation. Ultimately, that's all it is, and it's within the reach of everyone.

Most humans feel inadequate or less than deserving to actually experience an enlightened state of consciousness. This is a basic issue to be addressed and overcome in a true spiritual search.

We have all witnessed or done or thought things which are less than loving. But we have an opportunity to expand our mindsets and begin looking at ourselves and our world as part of an "Earth School" in which we have all agreed to participate. From there, we can approach a detachment in which various mindfulness practices, beginning with meditation, can allow messages from our heart centers to enter our ego-dominated minds.

The idea that we must overcome the perception of ourselves as permanently flawed sinners can seem daunting. We can start with the idea that this is just a belief like any other and, therefore, it can be changed. It is not an immutable truth, and the fact that we are not perfect while human can be accepted without the condemnation.

For those who want some tremendous insight into the inner-spirit perspective of our lives, I recommend reading *Emmanuel's Books I, II, and III.* In these metaphysical classics, a teacher named Emmanuel speaks through two American authors, Pat Rodegast and Judith Stanton, and emphasizes that, *"who you are is a necessary step to who you will be."*

Another key teaching by Emmanuel is also worthy of mention:

> *"All true spiritual teachers in any country and in any faith have served the great purpose of directing human consciousness individually and collectively to the God within."*[4]

One of the most influential Eastern mystics to have brought these spiritual traditions to the Western world was Paramahansa

Yogananda. His book, *Autobiography of a Yogi*, is truly an astounding life story. He is credited with bringing yogic traditions to the United States and greatly expanding our understandings and practice of these traditions. In the book, he made a most interesting comment on the topic of enlightenment:

> *"There is no insuperable obstacle in merging the human with the divine. No such barrier exists, I came to understand, save in man's spiritual un-adventurousness."*[5]

So, what is the greatest obstacle to experiencing this reality of enlightenment? Tolle weighed in on that subject:

> *"Identification with the mind, which causes thought to become compulsive… This incessant mental noise prevents you from finding that realm of inner stillness that is inseparable from Being. It also creates a false mind-made self that casts a shadow of fear and suffering."*[6]

This realm of inner stillness is a desired state of meditation. Often your personal higher self or "spirit self" is referred to as your "I AM "presence.

## The Intellect

Here's an idea about enlightenment that is startling, but also intriguing: *You are not your mind.*

In other words, our intellect is a vital part of us, but it doesn't encompass all of us. The reality is, each of us is a mind-body-spirit embodiment, more accurately thought of as a mind-body-spirit complex. Our minds are just one of the tools to be utilized by the totality of our being.

The thing about our intellect is that it's natural and instinctive; we can't help but use it. But our intellect comes from (and is supported by) the energy that brings us into being. Our intellect is based on spontaneous processes about which it knows nothing.

The way our intellect colors the events of our lives is directly affected by our belief structures. It's important to understand that events which the intellect views as non-supportive, based on its beliefs, may well be self-corrective to our overall self.[7]

Our beliefs also have serious ramifications for our intellect. According to traditional religion, the intellect at least got the assurance of survival after death in some type of heaven. Unfortunately, science took away this assurance with its assertion that nothing follows our death. This was, and is, a big blow.

## The Choice

Within this discussion, there are basically two approaches to living our lives.

The first approach is simply to let life happen. Whatever comes, we do the best we can. This leads fairly quickly to feeling more like a victim than a creator. At any rate, it implies a certain level of "fate" and "uncertainty" as primary causative factors, living as a kind of passenger along for the ride. Some rides end up being much easier than others, most apparently.

The second approach—which falls under the umbrella of enlightenment—is to embrace the idea that humans are responsible for everything that happens in their lives. This is true whether or not we can make sense of everything that we encounter in life from our limited human perspective.

As a start, we can ask ourselves what the events of our lives can teach us (or have taught us) and what we will choose to do with that. Additionally, we understand that, if we don't like something, we can examine and change our beliefs—consciously manifesting changes to an ongoing condition or situation.

Statements like the above can prompt many questions. As I contemplate these and the other subjects barely described in this book, I sincerely hope that anyone interested will obtain the source materials from which these quotes are drawn.

There is no substitute for the bigger picture and the ongoing support which these works provide as life progresses. But if you can even glimpse the majesty and simplicity of what is being said by the quoted passages, it can help change your view of both yourself and your reality.

***Notes:***

1. Tolle, Eckhart, *A New Earth: Awakening to Your Life's Purpose,* Plume-Penguin Publishing, 2006, p. 4.
2. Pierrakos, *Surrender to God Within*, op. cit., p. 182.
3. Young-Sowers, *Agartha*, op. cit. p. 98.
4. Rodegast, Pat, and Stanton, Judith, *Emmanuel's Book 1,* Bantam Books, New York, p. 67.
5. Yogananda, Paramahansa, *Autobiography of a Yogi*, Self-Realization Fellowship, Los Angeles, California, 1998.
6. Tolle, Eckhart, *The Power of Now*, op. cit., p. 11.
7. No one can read *The Nature of Personal Reality* by Jane Roberts/Seth and not understand the absolute centrality of each person's beliefs, as their beliefs directly influence the assessment of the events of their lives.

# CHAPTER 17
# MYSTICISM

*"No intellectual explanation can be a substitute for spiritual experience; it can at best prepare the ground for that experience. As spiritual experience involves more than can be grasped by the intellect, it is often described as a mystical experience. This is a direct realization (cognition) of the infinite."*
**—Meher Baba/ Mystic Teacher**

Mysticism, by definition, is the practice of becoming one or having direct communication with a divine source through some type of subjective experience.

With that said, the word "mysticism" is not a term with which many people associate themselves. Although we have records and insights provided by mystics for every age of recorded human history, most of us still see this state as somehow beyond us. We somehow don't feel qualified or equipped.

Right now is as good a time as any to disabuse ourselves of the feeling that we, personally, cannot experience a mystical state. *We can.*

As I discussed in the last chapter, many metaphysical teachers describe a spiritual or mystical experience as being an expansion of consciousness or an overwhelming experience of belonging. Their intent is to frame these experiences as something attainable and not beyond the scope of capacity for normal human beings.

## My Personal Encounters

In Chapter 8, I shared with you my own experience with states of expanded consciousness, relating mostly to my out-of-body experiences (OOBEs). Pretty much from the beginning of these encounters, I sensed benign presences accompanying me during the events. Sometimes they would intervene directly to turn me in one direction or another. In several instances, they assumed the role of wise and loving teachers or higher aspects of my being to aid me in what must be called a type of mystical experience.

The point I want to make is that I'm just as human as anyone has ever been, and I'm basically no different than you are. But I don't ever recall having these mystical experiences before opening up my mind and my belief structure to the possibility of their occurring to me and then pointing my intention at this goal.

I know I cannot begin to adequately communicate the overwhelming magnificence of such experiences, but I hope this account will come a little closer to capturing one of them.

Shortly after retiring from the Navy, I traveled to Oregon to visit my brother-in-law. He had purchased a large tract of wilderness land and a ranch house in that area, and he was keen to show me all parts of it via his all-terrain, four-wheel-drive vehicle.

We spent several hours going over extremely difficult terrain with constant jarring and physical discomfort. Given my background, this was not a challenging experience by itself, but it contributed to my subsequent feeling of discomfort after eating an evening meal. Shortly after eating, I promptly began vomiting until there was nothing left to come up. This led to a quiet evening and an early bedtime.

Sometime during the night, I became fully and consciously aware of being out of my body. I was wide awake in the scene with all my faculties functioning, and I was completely surrounded by an overwhelming, penetrating "light" which I somehow knew to also be conscious and loving.

This light was so overwhelming in its splendor that I felt its loving penetration into every cell of my being. As with a normal waking state, I had full conscious volition to do, think, or say anything I wanted, although I was also fully aware of my actual body asleep on the bed in the ranch guest bedroom.

Since the light was everywhere, there wasn't anywhere I wanted to be but in it. A type of ecstasy possessed me, and I realized that many of the questions which had been on my mind during my years of active spiritual endeavors simply weren't important. I was shown what seemed to me to be a long line of physical bodies which I understood were all related intimately to me. In this state of cell-deep exaltation, I felt I never wanted to leave.

At some point, I asked a question, which was "Can I come home?" The answer came immediately with a clearly audible voice and said, "Of course." With this, my ecstasy level rose beyond my ability to tolerate it, and I found myself immediately back in my body, wide awake, and in my bed. I got up and wrote down my experience.

I realize that description does little justice to this mystical experience, but it happened to me in just that way. It might seem simple, but it was dramatic and life-altering and unforgettable. I've had similar experiences over the years, and each one of them remains extremely important and valuable to me. I hope to be forever thankful for them.

## The Gateway

So, what is our role in opening ourselves up to this type of mystical experience? I will use an analogy:

The human is like an archer whose job is to take up the bow and aim the arrow at the desired target. Upon releasing the arrow, the archer's work is done. If the archer (human) is pointing the arrow (desire) at the target (divinity), it becomes the responsibility of divinity to provide the gift of enlightenment when the time is right. From the human side, our job is to not give up on the desire for direct and personal mystical contact.

In *The Law of One, Book III*, a channeled source named Ra explains this perspective:

> *"In the experiences of the mystical search for unity, these (time/space and space/time concepts) need never be considered, for they are part of an illusionary system. The seeker seeks The One. The One is to be sought, as we have said, by the balanced and self-accepting self, aware, both of its apparent distortions and its total perfection. Resting in this balanced awareness, the entity (mind-body-spirit complex) then opens the self to the universe which it is. The light energy of all things may then be attracted by this intense seeking, and wherever the inner seeking meets the attracted cosmic prana, realization of 'The One' takes place."*[1]

Eckhart Tolle also provides commentary on the phenomenon of mysticism:

*"To become conscious of Being, you need to reclaim consciousness from the mind. This is one of the most essential tasks on your spiritual journey. It will free vast amounts of consciousness that previously had been trapped in useless and compulsive thinking. A very effective way of doing this is simply to take the focus of your attention away from thinking and direct it into the body, where Being can be felt in the first instance as the invisible energy field that gives life to what you perceive as the physical body... The feeling of your inner body is formless, limitless, and unfathomable… Pay attention to whatever you can feel.*[2]

An English Anglo-Catholic writer known for her works about spiritual practices, Evelyn Underwood also provides additional insights to add texture to this definition:

*"(Mysticism is) the science or art of the spiritual life…the innate tendency of the human spirit towards complete harmony with the transcendental order, whatever be the theological formula under which that order is understood. That is, the true line of development of the highest form of human consciousness.*

*"Mysticism, then, is not an opinion; it is not a philosophy. It has nothing in common with the pursuit of occult knowledge. It is the name of that organic process which involves the perfect consummation of the Love of God: the achievement here and now of the immortal heritage of man. Or, if you like it better—for it means the same thing; it is the art of establishing his conscious relationship with the absolute."*[3]

## The Role of Energy

It is now generally understood that everything we perceive and everything that we posit to exist is composed of energy. Science and religion may differ on the prime cause of this energy but, from quantum theory on one pole to astrophysics on the other, everything from the most minute particle of matter to a super nova are capable of being described in terms of their energy content as a fundamental property.

From there, it's not a great reach to describe a human as fundamentally being energy in motion. The leap of faith is to see ourselves as an aspect of divinity having a human experience, and not as simply an energy creation cut off or isolated from our divine source.

One metaphysical principle is that all energy is neutral and, in our spectrum of vibration (which we refer to as "reality"), appears in its form as caused by each human's perception of it. The principle is that we are "co-creators" with the divine force which has placed us here as humans.

If you can accept this understanding as a basis for creative action through our thoughts and emotions, it's immediately obvious that the two poles are "fear" on one end and "love" or "trust" on the other. Whatever our mind is programmed to believe will dominate the events of our lives.

If we see the world as basically dangerous and mankind as little more than a thinking animal, we will draw to us exactly what these thoughts attract. Conversely, if we believe that we are divine in nature and personally live in a safe universe, this will be our overall experience.

This helps to explains the differences between the view of humanity held by people who label themselves "conservative" versus those who identify as "liberal." Neither is right or wrong, per se. Each position simply reflects the beliefs they hold and shows that their energy is focused in a different place.

## The Benefit of Observation

As a learning tool, each individual's life can be seen as simply a projection on a viewing screen which we refer to as "reality." An enlightened approach is simply to observe everything without judgment. As put by Edgar Cayce, it is to be "in this world but not of it." What Cayce is saying is that a truly advanced spiritual attitude is to view all events with a relaxed openness, detachment, and receptivity.

Meredith Young-Sowers/Mentor reinforces that thought:

*"All input having to do with spiritual awareness is communicated from the mental heart to the superconscious to await recognition by the conscious mind... Unless there is conscious interest in extracting a new piece of information from the database, the piece of understanding remains stored... Awareness is but a matter of opening the conscious floodgates and letting attunement flow in... The conscious program is that network of input which the conscious mind advances as reality... It may or may not be a true picture. Incoming data is analyzed in light of this program and is accepted or rejected accordingly."*[4]

## The Obstacles

Knowing the potential wonder of having a mystical experience, what keeps us from opening a channel to our divine source—God/Goddess/All That Is? Several items come up through various teachers as being impediments. Among these are feelings of personal guilt, religious dogmas and rules, and religious teachings that make believers feel they are "not good enough."

Mary-Margaret Moore/Bartholomew describes this beautifully:

> *"(There's a) fear of God: that we don't measure up; we are going to be destroyed, or be punished, or go to some 'dark area'—which sounds worse than annihilation. Thus, many people are no longer trying to open their channels to the divine. (There's) fear of being loved as you are now."*[5]

## The Journey

I can't possibly overstate the joy of having a mystical experience. There are no words to properly describe or define it. You simply have to choose to open yourself up to the possibility of having one and welcome it as part of your journey. The truth of the actual experience will speak for itself.[7]

I want to add some thoughts about the importance of gratitude. Spiritual teachers almost universally mention this as a key ingredient which opens the heart and is innate in an actual mystical experience. Look for things you appreciate, and cultivate an "attitude of gratitude." Focus on the good you have experienced. Make a list, if necessary, and review it often. The impact of this practice is felt directly by your mind, body, and spirit.

For anyone interested in spurring themselves on towards a personal mystical approach to divinity, I cannot think of a better book to begin with than *The Way of Paradox* by Father Cyprian Smith. He was a Benedictine monk living and teaching at Ampleforth Abbey in Yorkshire, England, when he wrote this book.

Father Cyprian Smith used the writings of a thirteenth century Christian mystic, Meister Eckhart, as a backdrop for his teaching on the direct approach to mystical experiences. He produced a truly life-changing book and thoughtful reflection on the human spiritual path, generally, and the obtainability of direct mystical experience, explicitly.[6]

Clearly both Father Cyprian Smith and Meister Eckhart believed that a direct ascent to conquer the mountain of mystical experience was not only feasible but attainable for anyone truly desiring it. The goal is nothing less than a fully embodied, conscious experience of the divine core of our being.

***Notes:***

1. Ra, *The Law of One, Book III*, Whitford Press, 1982, p. 51.
2. Tolle, Eckhart, *The Power of Now*, New World Library, 1999, pp. 90-94.
3. Underhill, Evelyn, *Mysticism*, p. 80.
4. Young, *Agartha*, op. cit., pp. 90-91.
5. Moore, Mary-Margaret, *Bartholomew: From the Heart of a Gentle Brother,* High Mesa Press, 1987.
6. Smith, Cyprian OSB, *The Way of Paradox*, Darton, Longman and Todd LTD, London, 2007. After reading this book, I traveled to England in 2010 and Father Cyprian met with me for an afternoon's discussion, for which I will always remain very grateful. This gentle soul simply radiated the goodness we all would like to see in ourselves. To sum up, I said to Father Cyprian that he obviously had personal mystical leanings, so didn't he find it hard to stay within the dogmatic boundaries prescribed by the Catholic Church? Father Cyprian's answer was that he had given a lot of thought to

this issue, but that he had decided that he could best serve by helping change the Church from within. There was a big lesson in this for me.

7. For anyone who wishes to have a deeper understanding of the human capability to expand our normal range of consciousness, two outstanding books are Ken Wilber's *No Boundary* and *The Spectrum of Consciousness,* Quest Books, multiple years.

# CHAPTER 18
# CONSCIOUS MANIFESTATION

*"Reality is merely an illusion, albeit a very persistent one."*
**—Albert Einstein**

One pivotal concept in metaphysics is that we are each the creators of our reality, either consciously through understanding this fact, or unconsciously based upon our belief structures. While this idea was challenging for me at first, it now seems so obvious that I'm amazed it isn't more widely understood. Many people do now embrace the concept, with positive results in their lives.

Moving toward taking self-responsibility in life involves contemplating the thought that the events of our lives are not accidents. If they are not accidents, then they have a cause. If they have a cause that we personally influence in some way, then obviously we should be truly interested in understanding more about how this works.

Conscious manifestation, then, is about setting a clear intention, giving specific direction to your desire, believing you have the power to make your vision a reality, and taking action to make it happen.

Two quotes from Jane Roberts/Seth help to set the scene:

*"Many of you believe that it is safe to make a nuclear bomb, but that it is insane to use your dreams as another method of manipulating daily life; or that it is all right to be consciously aware of your viruses, wars, and disasters, but that it is* <u>*not*</u> *all right to be consciously aware of other portions of the self that could solve such problems.*

*"The idea, then, is not to annihilate normal consciousness, but quite literally to expand it by bringing into its focus other levels of reality that it can indeed intrinsically perceive and utilize."*[1]

*"If you do not like a television program, you can switch to another with a mere flick of the wrist. If you do not like your own physical experience, you can also change to another, more beneficial station—but only if you recognize the fact that you are the producer."*[2]

## Conscious Co-Creation

This brings us to a major topic among many metaphysical teachers. How can we as human beings consciously create or, more appropriately put, consciously co-create with the divine force, to affect the challenges and outcomes in our lives?

I believe that humanity's next spiritual goal is to learn to create consciously what we now create largely unconsciously.

Wise words in an article from author Rochelle Diane Sparrow underscore this point:

> *"Up to now you have discounted your intention as meaningless to your own life. However, it is your intention and not 'fate,' as you have defined it, that has created your world. Know that if you look at yourselves with great and exacting clarity, what you will discover is a great connection to the Source that has been ever present but not acknowledged."*[3]

## Key Factors

Two fundamental points of departure are these statements from Jane Roberts: "Beliefs create reality" and "The present is the point of power."[4]

Unpackaged, these statements refer to the assertion that the fundamental building blocks are our beliefs, which affect our thoughts, which determine our emotions, which lead to the actual events in our lives. And furthermore, our beliefs are not truths; they are simply thoughts which we continually repeat to ourselves.

These repetitive thought patterns can and do change all the time. As an example, when you were little, you didn't think you could cross the road or dive into a swimming pool. Then one day you did, and your beliefs on that subject changed. The fact is, each person's beliefs are the foundation for the reality they experience in their lives.

The second statement ("The present is the point of power") also makes good sense. Any changes we wish to make to ourselves or to our minds must be done in the present from our current point of being. The past is in the past, and the future is yet to come.

Our present is the result of a combination of our actions and beliefs up to this exact moment. From this point on, we project those choices, plus any new ones, into each future "present" moment. The contents of our projections, based largely on our emotions and beliefs, could not be more important.

## Strategies

At the risk of simplifying an extremely important topic too much, I will just outline a few thoughts. We can understand (and change if we want to) our personal beliefs by minimally two basic methods:

1. By consciously examining our beliefs, listing them out one by one, and using our reasoning abilities (mind) to act as a type of flashlight shining on one belief after another that we might not normally focus on.
2. Or by analyzing life's events as they happen and the emotions they raise within us. Then asking, "What must I believe to be experiencing this or that emotion?"

The major components of conscious efforts at manifestation are:

- Desire
- Imagination
- Expectancy

Each one of these is a full topic of study and excellently discussed by the spiritual teachers listed at the end of this book.

A favorite teacher of mine, Esther Hicks/Abraham, now has a worldwide support base of people positively influenced by the Abraham teachings. In their simplest form, Abraham says that our desires appear (line up) all the time. We are desiring machines.

We always desire something. Even a desire not to desire anything for ourselves is a desire.

Abraham puts forth these three steps for conscious manifestation.

Step One is getting clear on your desires. What is it that you really want?

Step Two is automatic. The universe ("All That Is") hears us and registers every desire.

Step Three involves doing the work. We must allow the desire into our lives. Essentially this often means getting out of our own way with regard to our limiting thoughts and beliefs about the desired outcome. Put simply, if you desire a new car, you can't spend your time thinking about all the reasons you can't have one.[5]

## Visualization

As mentioned, a fundamental metaphysical precept is that we get whatever we concentrate on. There is no other main rule, according to all metaphysical teachers discussing this subject.

Put in very mundane terms, legendary automaker Henry Ford was quoted as saying:

*"If you think you can, you can. If you think you can't, you can't."*

Summing it up, every event in our lives triggers an emotion which we can examine. Every emotion comes from a belief or a series of beliefs which we hold.

When visualizing a desired goal or outcome, visualize the essence of what you want to occur, but don't get bogged down in details.

The Jach Pursel/Lazaris materials provide an excellent description of the process of conscious manifestation. They also offer detailed lists of aspects of desire, imagination, and expectancy to uncover any hidden beliefs/emotions which can hinder manifestation of the desired outcome.

Before leaving this topic, the full-trance channel Eva Pierrakos (who shared the lessons from Teacher) points out several important things to keep in mind.

*"What is your aim in life? How far do you wish to go? To just remove a few symptoms or to achieve total self-realization? In this latter regard, total commitment brings total possibilities.*

*"Find the exact point where your positive wishes are blocked, and then question what particular character defect does not permit you to abandon a self-destructive, self-denying attitude. State clearly that you wish to find it. Two major issue areas are fear and shame."*[6]

In her book, *Creating Union*, Pierrakos/Teacher also states:

*"There are two fundamental principles through which the creative process works. The* ***first*** *is activation (desire, imagination, expectancy related); the* ***other*** *is getting out of the way and 'letting it happen.' Direct creation is always an expression of consciousness.*

*"The masculine (creative) and the feminine (attitude of 'letting be' or 'receptive') operate together. 'Letting be' is a pulsating, involuntary movement or patience, and trustful waiting."*[7]

Pierrakos adds that nothing can be created without both principles at work.

## Perceptions

Our individual point of view determines our perspective, which also defines the focus of our perception. Author Saemmi Muth channels comments on this situation:

> *"You have accepted the premise that human beings at large require a rigid discipline to contain them, to civilize them, so to speak. We suggest to you that this very deeply ingrained belief is the strongest element in continuing to keep the 'them/us' issues alive. We suggest to you that control issues thrive on your own sense of powerlessness to change or alter your own response to life... We suggest to you that cause and effect are not separate issues; they are reactions to vibrations that express thought and response."*[8]

Pierrakos/Teacher summarizes this point with great clarity:

> *"The moment you can see the level in you where your concepts, intentions, and attitudes create your life circumstances, you have your key to create a different and more desirable life."*[9]

## Framing the Concept of Reality

On the subject of creating our own reality, the discussion would not be complete without mentioning the messages of Seth through Jane Roberts in the book called, *The Magical Approach.* Seth maintains that this approach to understanding our situation is actually the closest to how things that we perceive as "real" actually occur.

Seth uses the terms "Framework One" and "Framework Two" to help explain this concept.

**Framework One** is simply a descriptor for "reality" as we perceive it with our senses. **Framework Two** describes the overarching subjective milieu in which our "reality" exists. We can think of Framework Two as both divinely inspired and positively biased to the well-being and growth of everything appearing in Framework One. These two Frameworks are always intertwined, but they can be analyzed separately to provide an intellectual and intuitive understanding.

Seth's "magical approach" to understanding and experiencing our reality is described as being "the adult version of childhood knowledge, the human version of animal's knowledge, the conscious version of 'unconscious' comprehension."[10]

Understanding the core principles of this magical approach to reality is immensely valuable. The term *magical* in this context signifies a holistic way of perceiving personal reality, addressing challenges and obstacles, and achieving objectives by harnessing all the mental and spiritual resources available to us in the most natural manner.

Our cultural conditioning often leads us to rely on reasoning things out, sometimes causing us to overlook or be unaware of the inherent gifts and support that each human being possesses. In essence, the magical approach is, in fact, the natural approach that we can embrace and trust to provide substantial assistance throughout our life's journey. A central tenet of this approach is that, with the right attitude and focused attention, we can attract the events and resources necessary for a constructive and positive life—another way to access conscious manifestation.

This concept is relatively easy to grasp. As spiritual beings fundamentally composed of energy within physical form, our overall energy signature naturally draws certain experiences while repelling others. By shifting our focal point and altering what we consider significant, we can effectively modify our energy signature.

The foundation of this perspective on reality is rooted in simple truths. The following paragraphs contain a paraphrased synopsis from Seth that further illuminate these principles:

> *The magical perspective assumes, in its simplest form, that every individual's life will naturally unfold, develop, and mature in harmony with their unique environment. This may seem straightforward. However, these beliefs are inherent at the cellular level, imprinted within each chromosome and atom. They instill an innate faith that permeates all living beings, from the tiniest cell to every strand of hair on one's head. These deeply ingrained convictions serve a vital biological purpose, propelling growth and development.*
>
> *You manifest what you focus on. There exists no other fundamental rule.*
>
> *True power resides in the imagination that dares to envision the yet-to-be.*[11]

Moving from concept to action is the key to creating our reality. Inspired by Seth, these four resolutions can help you take responsibility for generating that momentum:

1. *I will embrace and accept myself fully, acknowledging my qualities, talents, preferences, strengths, weaknesses, inclinations, and aversions; recognizing that these aspects make up my unique individuality and are bestowed upon me with purpose.*

2. *I will celebrate and take pride in my achievements. I will be just as enthusiastic in acknowledging and remembering these accomplishments as I have been in cataloging my failures or lack of success.*
3. *I will keep in mind the creative framework within which my existence unfolds. I will hold the possibilities, potentials, apparent miracles, and spontaneous joys of Framework Two in my awareness, ensuring that the doors to a creative life remain wide open.*
4. *I will understand that the future is a realm of probabilities. In the context of everyday experience, it contains nothing concrete. It is a blank canvas awaiting my feelings and thoughts to shape it. Consequently, I will plan for achievements and successes, guided by the understanding that nothing can exist in the future that I do not wish to manifest there.*[12]

I find that reviewing my life regularly with Seth's list of resolutions in mind is extremely supportive. Focusing on the above four points as they relate to us and the events of our lives personally is a therapy in itself.

Seth's list is significant in that he is proposing that we completely alter our focus of depending solely on our intellects for problem solving. The rational view of life has separated us from a sense of connection to our own power source. Historically, when man identified himself more with his soul, he actually gave himself more leeway for psychological support than someone relying on the rational scientific belief that we have no soul.

What we are actually doing is opening up to a free flow of information from other levels of our being, which are always available. There are practical and far-reaching effects of this change in mindset, as Seth explains:

*"Now when you understand that intellectually, then the intellect can take it for granted that its own information is not all the information you possess. It can realize that its own knowledge represents the tip of the iceberg. As you apply that realization to your life you begin to realize furthermore that in practical terms you are indeed supported by a greater body of knowledge than you consciously realize, and by the magical, spontaneous fountain of action that forms your existence....* ***The intellect can then realize that it does not have to go it all alone. Everything does not have to be reasoned out, even to be understood."***[13]

This is so important when taking into account the propensity of our intellects to often display paranoid tendencies when it feels that it must solve all of our personal problems by itself alone, and particularly when it contemplates worldwide predicaments. When left on its own, our intellect often imagines that "the worst is yet to come" and proceeds from that perspective.

You can see that the thrust of these ideas on a more open-minded approach to problem solving is both life-affirming and supportive of human beings as more than simple chemical accidents or a flawed species created to suffer until it prays enough or changes enough to please a judging God.

Whether you open up to Seth's "magical approach" to reality or think of our human experience in any other way, it's overwhelmingly important to decide whether a human's life has meaning or not. If we can find our way to believing that it does—through any method—then we are moving forward on a conscious spiritual path and greater happiness in life.

## Creating My Own Reality

My personal experiences with conscious manifestation have resulted in many of my desired goals coming directly to fruition. In other instances, my efforts led to different results which I ultimately felt were better for me than what I had originally intended.

I will use just one example of the latter outcome. Following my tour as Commanding Officer of SEAL Team One, I decided I wanted to stay in San Diego and be assigned as a "Commodore" of the Special Operations Boat Units there. The title of "Commodore" simply refers to people who have more than one command under their direct supervision. I began the work to visualize this outcome. Instead, as I have discussed earlier in this book, I received orders to Key West for a joint command in a less prestigious job.

As it turned out, the years spent in Key West were some of the happiest and most meaningful for Heather and me. When my superior officer there retired, I had the opportunity for advancement—which ended up being a major promotion. That taught me an important lesson: I should continue with my conscious manifestation work, but without judging the ultimate outcome prematurely.

A quote from the prolific American author James Michener comes to mind:

> *"The permanent temptation in life is to confuse dreams with reality. The permanent defeat comes when dreams are surrendered to reality."*

If you are interested in this topic, I highly recommend reading the excellent source materials. Then simply begin practicing, keeping in mind that your basic beliefs on the subject of any desired goal should take precedence and accompany the actual work you do.

I will close this chapter with a short excerpt by Emmanuel, one of my favorite spiritual teachers:

> *"Right now, in this particular life,*
> *nothing exists beyond the moment.*
> *The next moment awaits your creation.*
> *With your next inhalation,*
> *you bring forth whatever you allow*
> *through the composite performance*
> *of what you have already created,*
> *what you allow to be present now,*
> *and the capacity for Love you choose."*[14]

Every human takes a stand in believing that we either create our personal realities or we don't. The challenge here is to dig into this material and then decide for yourself. The quotes in this chapter are literally just the tip of a massive iceberg of expanded understanding about conscious manifestation and the metaphysical philosophy. I hope you'll spend some time with them.

The blessing to be found from this book is not in its details. It comes when you probe deeply enough into the sources referenced here to arrive at an understanding of who and what we really are: an aspect of God having a purposeful human existence.

This is the feeling of coming home. This is the knowing that we have never been cut off or separate from the Source. Each of us are who we are for a reason. This is the feeling of strength and active support in the spiritual leg of a person's supporting mind-body-spirit stool.

***Notes:***

1. Roberts, Jane, *The Nature of the Psyche: Its Human Expression*, Amber-Allen Publishing, 1995, p. 46.
2. Roberts, Jane, ibid., p. 21.
3. Sparrow, Rochelle Diane, "You See with the Eyes of the Source," *Sedona Journal of Emergence,* May 2003, p. 48.
4. Roberts, *The Nature of Personal Reality*, op. cit.
5. Hicks, Esther and Jerry, *Ask and It Is Given*, op. cit.
6. Pierrakos, Eva, *Surrender to God Within*, Pathwork Press, 1997, p. 90
7. Pierrakos, Eva, *Creating Union*, Pathwork Press, 1993, pp. 13-19.
8. Muth, Saemmi, "Embracing Your Christed Resonance," *Sedona Journal of Emergence,* February 1996, pp. 14-15.
9. Pierrakos, *Surrender to God Within*, op. cit., p. 176.
10. Roberts, *Dreams (Volume II),* op. cit., p. 527.
11. Roberts, *Dreams (Volume I),* op. cit., pp. 181-183.
12. Roberts, ibid., p. 185.
13. Roberts, *The Magical Approach,* Amber-Allen, 1995, p. 16.
14. Rodegast, Pat, and Stanton, Judith, *Emmanuel's Book III*, Bantam Books, 1994, p. 85.

# CHAPTER 19
# TAKING THE NEXT STEPS

*"Be not afraid of growing slowly; be only afraid of standing still."*
**—Chinese Proverb**

Since you've made it to this point in the book, I think it's fair to ask you a question: What do you think the path looks like on *your* spiritual journey going forward?

I've shared how my experiences led me to embrace the principles of metaphysics. As I stated from the beginning, that might not be the answer for everyone. But if you are intrigued by this information, I want to provide some specific steps you can take to further explore this concept and embark on your own spiritual journey.

To be clear, spirituality doesn't involve a formula. But there are some things you can do to prepare your mind and your heart for the wonders of a new perspective.

## Assess the Starting Point

The best place to start is exactly where you are in life right now. To the extent that your environment, work, relationships, and finances are stable and positive, you can be pretty sure that your current belief structure is solid and supportive. But if you want to make improvements in certain aspects of your life, you can begin by examining your beliefs in these areas to see whether or not they are serving you.

Jane Roberts/Seth asserts that everyone intuitively is looking to fulfill their innate capacities, not just survive. The bigger principle involves all of life.

> *"In physical reality, life is the name of the game—and the game is based on value fulfillment. That means simply that each form of life seeks towards the fulfillment and unfolding of all of the capacities that it senses within its living framework, knowing that in individual fulfillment each other species of life is also benefitted."*[1]

## Remember Metaphysics 101

I couldn't possibly begin to cover all the different aspects of metaphysics in this book, but I hope I've articulated some of the key beliefs that form the foundation of this philosophy. Keeping these in mind as you continue your journey can be helpful, as well as comforting. As a quick refresher:

- **You are a part of the divine source having a physical learning experience.**

  Being human means that the physical portion of ourselves is and always will be imperfect, but the spiritual core of our being has never been separate from the whole, from the divine source by whatever name. Our biggest personal challenge is learning to listen to our inner being (our higher self).

- **Your life has a purpose.**
  All that is required of each of us is a faithful seeking of the truth that life has meaning and that each of us has a role to play in it—or we wouldn't be here. So if we're on this earth, we still have some learning or service to others left to do.

- **You were born in a state of grace.**
  We are all born in a state of grace, live in a state of grace, and will die in a state of grace. Simply changing our belief that man is not the one flawed species in an otherwise perfect natural order of things can truly be life affirming and life changing.

- **You are energy in the form of mass, designed to move forward.**
  Regardless of where we are on our spiritual path, resting on our oars is not the answer. We need to learn to rely on our divine source and to help ourselves throughout life by our own efforts. Take the next step.

- **You are in control of creating the life you want.**
  We have the personal power to change ourselves and the outcomes we project into the world. We have access to tools like conscious manifestation and visualization that can help us mold the reality we want to create. Essentially, we draw life's experiences to us based on our concentration, beliefs, and expectations.

## Commit to Doing the Work

Many years ago, I saw a bumper sticker on a car referring to a huge mountain outside of Taos, New Mexico:

*"Quit whining; just ski it."*

At some point, we have to stop evaluating the various aspects of a spiritual journey and…just do it. Take the first step.

An excellent quote by John C. Maxwell is: "You will never change your life until you change something you do daily."

Make it a daily habit to practice a personally wholesome discipline, focusing on the well-being of your mind, body, and spirit. Be gentle with yourself. Choose simple happiness through better choices and actions. And do whatever is necessary to arrive at the full conscious understanding and awareness that life has meaning—and we each have a role to play in it.

We have a right and a responsibility to be here on this planet, and life will show us what we need to learn. We are not responsible for anyone else's challenges, but we are responsible for our own. Put yourself in a position to do well at that task. Then move forward at whatever pace works for you.

## Meditate

*Noise*
*Is a cruel ruler,*
*Who is always imposing*
*Curfews,*
*While stillness and quiet*
*Break open the vintage Bottles,*
*Awake the real Band.*
**—Hafiz, *The Gift***

An important starting point for a personal spiritual search is the practice of meditation. For clarity, think of prayer as talking to God, while meditation is listening to God.

Yogis and spiritual teachers in many parts of the world have been practitioners and teachers of the value of meditation for thousands of years. Although the topic was once a matter of opinion, science now has definitive proof that meditation beneficially changes the brain waves of the meditator.

If you search for information about meditation and meditative techniques, you'll discover a voluminous amount of material. In general, there are *many* ways to meditate, but there are no *wrong* ways.

You can think of meditation as the quieting of your complete self and focusing on an item or single thought. Anything can serve as a meditation, such as a taking a walk in nature, listening to music, or looking at the night sky. Even the simple act of washing and drying dishes with focus and full consciousness could be an act of meditation. Whatever centers you in well-being and minimizes the chatter of the intellect is just fine.

The aim of meditation is to seek a balanced mind, which has an offshoot of increased feelings of harmony, wellness, joy, and a more grounded appreciation of ourselves. The only expectation is that it should be an enjoyable experience leading to a heightened sense of presence and calm.

One of the most famous spiritual teachers, Deepak Chopra, M.D., has reached and influenced millions of people throughout the world. He has very interestingly re-coined the acronym "RPM" (which typically stands for "Revolutions Per Minute") to stand for "Rise, Pee, and Meditate." In terms of an instruction for life, it can't get any simpler.

Building on Chopra's advice for RPM, take a few minutes for yourself early in the morning and/or just before bedtime. Read a bit of whatever spiritual material interests and uplifts you to help set the tone for your day or your dreams. This is a basic practice that has been followed by humans for millenniums.

A bedrock foundation of your meditation practice is to accept yourself, while forgiving yourself and all others. It doesn't mean that you are perfect or that you don't have sincere remorse for some of your thoughts and actions. It does mean accepting that we are all created from love and are here to learn from the experiences of this life. Embrace the qualities of nonjudgment, forgiveness, and gratitude.

In your meditation time, focus on what is going right in your life, not on what is wrong. Remember that thoughts create emotions, and repetitive thoughts create beliefs. Understand that your mind controls you much more than you control it. That alone is a great reason to take up meditation!

As with most beneficial habits, the secret of progress in meditation is regular practice. You can't get into better physical shape without working out regularly, and you can't get into better spiritual shape without a regular practice of meditation.

### *Focus*

Winston Churchill was quoted in one of his biographies as saying that he generally had about six things on his mind which were bothering him at any time. The way he dealt with them was *to prioritize*. His thought process likely went something like this:

> *Of the six things worrying me, I can't do anything about two of them. Another two will probably resolve themselves over time. But I can take action on the other two, and that will be my focus.*

This approach is generally applicable and helpful to many of the issues which bother us. Seeking to maintain our focus means being present in the moment and giving our full attention to whatever is right in front of us. That's great advice for life and for pursuing a spiritual path. It definitely came in handy during my military service.

Navy SEALs had to master a wide range of skills, which included becoming parachutist skydivers. The act of parachuting from an airplane produces an extreme amount of adrenaline, and it can be overwhelming if all aspects of the dive are colliding in your mind at once.

Here's an example to illustrate that point. You start by carefully packing your parachute. But once that is finished, you forget about whether it was done properly and trust it will open when you need it. Next, you load the plane and check your equipment. You need every fastener to be fastened and all items and equipment present and working. Then you block that out of your mind.

Next, you get ready to exit the airplane. All your thoughts should now be on a proper and safe exit, which can be particularly difficult if a big group is exiting simultaneously. Once you're falling through the air, your entire focus is reaching a stable position and, perhaps, entering a formation if you're performing in-flight link-ups or other maneuvers.

Then comes the moment to slow down the freefall. All your mental focus should be on maintaining the proper body position and opening the parachute at the right time. After pulling the rip cord, the only thing to think about is whether you have a fully functioning parachute over your head. If not, you begin your emergency procedures.

Once you prepare to touch down on land or water, your priority is to get there successfully without injury. And finally, you shift all your mental energy to get out of your parachute harness before the wind drags you dangerously forward or you drown.

The whole reason for describing that scenario is to demonstrate the necessity of taking on challenges in life sequentially. Separate out the things you can control from the things you can't. Don't allow yourself to become overwhelmed by worrying about every one of them at the same time. Just focus on doing the next, right thing.

This idea transcends cultural boundaries. The Russians have a practical saying:

*"Shoot the wolves closest to the sled first!"* The Spanish philosophy is also mentally liberating: *"If the problem has a solution, what are you worried about? And if the problem doesn't have a solution, what are you worried about?"*

Focus quite literally means paying primary attention to what is at hand. Be a gentle observer rather than someone who jumps into immediate reaction mode. Look for creative solutions to issues rather than immediately zoning out with "knee-jerk" reactions.

## Track What's Working

A very interesting book with a great approach to finding your spiritual path is called *The Lion Tracker's Guide to Life* by South African author Boyd Varty. He is also a real-life lion tracker who uses his on-the-job knowledge to help people focus on learning life's lessons. He cleverly points out the wisdom that comes from this common, life-coaching conversation:

Coach: *"How does that make you feel?"*
Subject: *"Terrible."*
Coach: *"Well then, don't do it."*

There is a brilliant simplicity in this approach. Track what makes you feel good and bring more of it into your life. Notice what makes you feel lousy and do less of it.

If you're in a place where things aren't going well, go back over the track of your life to the spot when you felt great about it. Be invested in the discovery rather than the outcome, and recognize that occasionally getting lost is part of the process. Follow the tracks, one after the other, until you reach the last clear track. Look for information there—how would taking a different path have changed where you are today? How can you get back to that?

Enter a fluid process of rediscovery and feedback. Welcome this feedback, both good and bad. Open your focus, and examine your beliefs. Follow your hunches. And remember that the path of "not here" is part of the path of "here."

## Trust Yourself

As you pursue your spiritual journey, I encourage you to trust your impulses and use your intuition, which is like your "personal guide dog." And perhaps the first rule of everything we endeavor to do is to pay attention to messages from all three legs of your mind-body-spirit support team.

Sir Laurens Van Der Post, a South African writer, commented on this idea:

> *"Meaning transfigures all… Once what you are living and what you are doing has meaning for you, it is irrelevant whether you are happy or unhappy. You're content. You're not alone in your spirit. You belong."*[2]

For those who can accept the premise that we are creators of our own personal realities, this becomes a major step towards healing the psyche—even if specific events aren't ever going to be fully understood from a human perspective. Accepting responsibility for the life we have created, and that we continue creating with all of its experiences, is redemptive.

We are given free will to choose for ourselves, and we get to live with the results of our "world view" choice as a growth tool. It is a blessing, not a curse. It requires both patience and flexibility to follow our experiences where they lead with the knowledge that we have inner guidance if we will only use it. Trust that you can figure out the way.

We are standing in our power when we align with the highest parts of ourselves while acknowledging both our humanity and our divinity.

## Final Thoughts

Opening yourself up to a broader paradigm doesn't have to be difficult. If you are dedicated to moving forward on your spiritual path, many of the actions I've mentioned can help you prepare for greater success. As succinctly put by Jane Roberts/Seth:

> *"It is not a matter of outlining a whole new series of methods that will allow you to increase your psychic abilities, or remember your dreams, or to perform out-of-body gymnastics. It is rather a question or a matter of completely altering your approach to life, so that you no longer block out such natural spontaneous activity."*[3]

It's an ongoing process rather than a destination, so find the confidence to keep moving forward. That concept reminds me of this interaction:

> A famous mystic was once asked by a pupil: *"How do I find enlightenment?"*
> The Master answered: *"Walk on."*

My other advice is to pay attention and stay open to whatever you find, even if it's not what you expect. Sometimes a story helps to illustrate that point.

There was a very religious family living in a river delta area whose house was flooded in a bad storm. They crawled to the roof and began praying to God for deliverance. The storm raged on, and the water continued to rise.

A man in a motorboat came by and offered to help them get off the roof. "Don't bother," they said. "God will take care of us." Later, a helicopter flew over them and a man descended down on a rope ladder to help them escape. Again, they said, "We're in God's hands. Don't worry about us!"

After refusing to leave the roof, the water rose quickly over the top of the house. They were swept away and drowned.

Arriving in Heaven, they say to St. Peter, "We're disappointed to be here so early. We were counting on God to help us!"

St. Peter gives a direct response: "Who do you think sent the motorboat and the helicopter?"

Sometimes we get what we need rather than what we expect. Remaining open to that idea can open up a world of new possibilities.

As you prepare to begin or continue your spiritual journey—whatever that looks like—I hope these ideas have added value for taking your next steps.

***<u>Notes:</u>***

1. Roberts, Jane, *Dreams, "Evolution," and Value Fulfillment (Volume II)*, Prentiss Hall, 1986, p. 316.
2. Sir Laurens Van Der Post quoted in *Divine Interventions* by Dan Millman, p 220.
3. Roberts, Jane, *Dreams (Volume II),* op. cit., p. 498. In addition to her 11 Seth novels, Jane Roberts had well over 1,000 sessions with Seth which were recorded. The first 510 sessions were subsequently published in book form with 9 total volumes as Roberts, Jane, *The Early Sessions*, New Awareness Network, 1997.

# CHAPTER 20
# THE MINDSET FOR SUCCESS

*"Life is everyone's military service."*
**-Unknown**

On our spiritual journey, it's helpful to nurture some emotions and feelings that will give you the best opportunity to move forward on a positive path. I continue to make these characteristics part of my life's guiding principles, and I realize I have experienced truly blessed results, both personally and professionally, as a direct result.

## Happiness

I don't think it's debatable to say that every normal human wants to be happy. But what will actually make us happy has long been the subject of much discussion—especially today, when polls tell us our individual happiness quotients are generally decreasing. There certainly are plenty of theories, but finding your own sense of happiness is crucial for your spiritual journey.

To get started, ask yourself: "What would make me happy?" For many people, the answers include such things as money, power, a fabulous vacation, or a great job. The fact is, the people who have more of the things on that list aren't necessarily any happier than the ones who have less.

You can try to narrow it down a bit by posing this question: "If everything in my life were exactly as I would most want it to be, what words would describe that state of being?" Naming the qualities associated with that state makes them more accessible.[1]

For me, I thought of words like interesting, exciting, fun, connection, purpose, challenge, vital, healing, and satisfied with the present. Your list will probably be different. While some qualities could be considered universally desirable and directly linked to happiness, we can conclude that there are a myriad of ways and possible options to experience these desirable states of being. Actually doing this exercise and playing with the idea is much more impactful than simply reading about it.

When I was still at the Naval Academy, I discovered books by author John Fowles, who greatly influenced my thinking at that time. In his book *The Aristos*, he describes humans as being "an infinite ever-lack"—endlessly preoccupied with wanting *more*. That's an interesting viewpoint to keep in mind when discussing happiness: As soon as we get what we *thought* we wanted, we want something additional or different.[2]

I've often heard it said that happiness isn't about getting all you want, but about enjoying all you've got. Perspective is everything. We can choose to increase our happiness every day by consciously deciding to focus more on feeling grateful for what we have. If we can accomplish that while having compassion for others and finding humor wherever we can, happiness will find us.

Several quotes from the book *Build the Life You Want* support that idea:

*"Happiness is not a destination. Happiness is a direction."*

And,

*"Happiness is a combination of enjoyment, satisfaction, and purpose."*[3]

American entrepreneur and investor Tim Ferriss has some targeted advice about increasing happiness in his book, *The 4-Hour Workweek*. His recommendation is to simply stop reading about or listening to the daily news—whether that be from TV, newspapers, radio, or streaming.

Ferriss points out that the great preponderance of news items focuses on problems, disasters, or tragic events over which we can do very little or nothing about. A constant diet of this type of mental input can lead to depression in those who take it in, both consciously and subconsciously. And if anything of true import occurs, someone will surely tell you about it.

This is a technique I have now practiced for many years, and I have seen an improvement in my daily mood. One of the happiest years of my life was when I was in Uruguay with no access to any formal news sources. I felt amazingly free from generalized worry all year long. Try it and see!

## Peace

The pace of forward movement on our spiritual journey is often determined by the type of emotions that are crowding our minds and our hearts. Are we filled with joy, peace, and forgiveness? Or are we weighed down with guilt, anger, doubt, and apathy?

Scientific studies clearly demonstrate the impact that optimistic thoughts and positive emotions have on our genes, including improved immune function, accelerated cellular repair, and stronger emotional resilience. Conversely, neuroscience has also proven the harmful effects on the body that result from perennially negative thoughts and emotions. The long-term side effects can include confusion and depression. At an extreme, they can lead to thoughts of, or actual, suicide.

The problem is, negative thinking can be a deeply ingrained habit. Despite that, it's a habit that's worthy of your efforts to break if you want to adjust the trajectory of your spiritual path. Change can be hard, but it's a prerequisite for growth.

A notable cliché is: *"If you always do what you did, you will always get what you always got."*[4]

This also reminds me of two sayings we had in the Navy:

1. *"Never wrestle with a pig. You both get dirty, and the pig likes it."*
2. *"The Law of Holes: When you find yourself in one, quit digging."*

Because of my experiences with PTSD after combat, I have often wrestled with the negative emotion of guilt, which can be crippling for the mind. The remedy for guilt is the ability to forgive yourself, which is a healing emotion. And an inability to forgive just adds salt to the wounds.

Modern therapy deals with how to ameliorate or eliminate these and other negative emotions that significantly impact people and their lives. Some groups are more vulnerable to extreme negative emotions. For instance, veterans have a higher rate of depression and suicide than the norm for adults. And the rates of depression and suicides are rising across the board, even for children and young adults.[4]

There can be multiple factors causing the mental pain that results in negative emotions. Called "stressors," these factors can be complex and unique to each individual. They can be of a continual nature or episodic, such as those reliving historical experiences of a disturbing nature, as evidenced in cases of PTSD.

In his book, *The Eye of the I (From Which Nothing Is Hidden),* scientist, mystic and author David R. Hawkins, M.D., does a wonderful job of outlining specific levels of human emotions. He describes the emotions at the very low end of the scale (which include things such as guilt, shame, apathy, grief, and fear) to those at the upper end of the scale (such as acceptance, love, joy, peace, and enlightenment).

For reference, guilt ranks lower on the scale than apathy and hatred.

Hawkins highlights our ability to identify where we currently are on the emotional scale, and then he provides the steps we can take to consciously move our emotions higher up.[5]

It's very difficult to move ourselves from a negative emotion like guilt to one of joy or peace in one giant leap. But what is clearly doable is to move up the emotional ladder, one step at a time. Hawkins shares specific and functional techniques to harness the mind in making those changes, and he does an excellent job correlating the spiritual and scientific aspects of the mind's functions as affected by states of consciousness.

To be fair, humans can't completely eliminate all negative emotions. Some of our thoughts and actions will inevitably be based in fear rather than love. But if we didn't have that continuum from dark to light, everything would simply be one color. That would leave us color blind. Contrast is innate in our learning experience, so accept that fact and pick your personal high road to growth.

Just keep in mind that this change process isn't a one-time event. It's a journey rather than a destination. It's active and ongoing.

This parable helps to highlight that concept.

*A man said he felt like he had two dogs living and fighting inside him. One was angry, sullen, and resentful. The other was happy and loving. Which dog will win?*

*Answer: The one that you feed.*

This is the crux of conclusions by neuroscience concerning the brain's propensity to create neural pathways which link thoughts and emotions. When the after-effects of trauma have created negative neural pathway links to related states of mental and emotional distress, reversing the impact takes deliberate action.

We have to work to create positive neural linkages that allow us to essentially change "tracks." Instead of finding ourselves on a negatively repeating loop, we need to feed the happy, loving dog—and do it often.

We do have the choice to be intentional about discarding the negative emotions when we can, which creates a different lens through which to see our reality—one that looks more supportive, happy, and secure. Even changing one belief can alter our mind-body-spirit experience of reality.

For some of the clearest and most straightforward directions about how to improve your mental state, the Esther Hicks/Abraham material is overwhelmingly impactful. The Abraham teachings say that we can elevate our mood by focusing our mental energy on a positive subject for a little as seventeen seconds. That concept has been life-changing for many people.[6]

## Self-Love

Our path toward spiritual enlightenment involves the cornerstone issue of self-love. This is something many of us need to continually work on. Acknowledging both what we perceive of as our shortcomings, as well as our better attributes, with the same loving acceptance leads to an ability to love all of ourselves as we are.

Jane Roberts/Seth also explain the simplicity of this idea:

> *"Attending to the life that you have with love, beginning 'where you are,' will best allow you such a feeling for your own meaning… What do I mean by such attention? Attention to the moment as it is presented. Attention to the table of rich reality as it appears before you. Attention to the kind of person you are, and to the loving appreciation of your own uniqueness. To attend to your life in such a fashion brings you into a clearer communication with the inner action of your own existence… Attend to what is directly before you."*[7]

If you're searching for more self-love and acceptance in your life, I highly recommend a book by American sociologist and author Martha Beck called *The Way of Integrity*. The word "integrity" in this sense refers to "wholeness" or finding your path to your true self. Many people feel stuck by lifelong negative patterns or, in more severe cases, to feelings of depression and hopelessness. This book is actually a very effective roadmap for those who want to determine how close or far away they are to "wholeness" and how to love themselves along the way.

The second book that I recommend in this regard is *Whole Brain Living* by Harvard neuroscientist Jill Bolte Taylor, Ph.D.

Taylor suffered a severe stroke and lost all her left-brain cognitive functions for several years, so that her remaining right-brain functions became dominant. As a scientist, she then used her own body as the subject of her research. Her story and her personal experiences have resulted in the most-listened-to TED talk of all time and made her internationally famous for her first book, *My Stroke of Insight.*

In very brief summary, Taylor describes that each of the four main lobes of our brains have different primary functions and purposes that can be characterized as personalities or "characters" with unique reactions to the various events of our lives. While the four lobes of our brain should work together, the left side lobes often take control to our detriment. The fact that we can have conscious control over which of the lobes we allow to dominate in a given situation is truly mind expanding.

## Compassion

The gift of compassion is not an equal-opportunity characteristic. Some people have a lot of it. Others don't seem to have much at all. But when we arrive at a modicum of actual spirituality, compassion is one of the byproducts. Although it may sound "soft," compassion is not a wimpy emotion. It arises from emotional balance and strength, and it is a vital emotion of spiritual growth.

So, what is it exactly? Compassion is the ability to recognize the suffering, struggle, and tests others go through on their evolutionary journeys. It's not weak or passive. It knows when to approach and when to give space. It understands human motivation and consequences. It does not engage in entanglement and victimhood, which are not compassionate but delusional.

Compassion recognizes that all humans have tests and obstacles. It understands that we each have developmental needs, and our individual roles and responsibilities are challenging in themselves. It supports others in the recognition of the unalterable spiritual nature of all human beings. And, in its essence, compassion is love without negative emotional attachments.[8]

Sometimes ancient wisdom is just as meaningful today:

*"Be kind, for everyone you meet is fighting a hard battle."*
**—Philo of Alexandria**

Compassion is based on an individual's belief structure, so any needed work on strengthening and expanding this emotion should begin with an examination of personal beliefs.

Recognizing that all of the above items can relate directly to becoming a happier person as you face life challenges, they also lead to the conclusion that being happy is a decision, not a given over which we have no control.

Integrating active spirituality into one's life clearly affects personal decision-making for issues big and small. In my case, I made a decision upon leaving the Navy to look for business opportunities which I felt would be beneficial to our world overall. I gravitated to looking for inventions which I felt met this criterion and could be scaled up into actual businesses.

My personal relationships with friends, colleagues, and employees also changed for the better as I began to view everyone in a more compassionate light. Certainly, the anxiety to excel which motivated me in my early years was tempered by seeing myself as a fellow spiritual traveler to every other human being.

## Curiosity

For those who feel lost or alienated in their life paths, there is currently a lot of talk about "finding your passion." That's good advice for someone who is passionate about *something*. But for others, that might seem daunting.

My best advice is to follow your "curiosity" or a series of interests in whatever direction they lead. Curiosity can be seen as a steady, gentle, kinder friend than passion, particularly for people who aren't sure where their passion lies. It is less demanding up front and doesn't require a certainty about a destination. It is easier to do and will eventually lead to a path of meaning. A simple delight in investigating the miraculous beauty of life and landscapes on our planet can start a healing process.

## Hope

One of the most important qualities we can have on our spiritual journey is hope. Simply defined, hope is to want something to happen or to be true with the expectation of a positive outcome. Put another way, hope is the feeling that things can get better in our future, even if the present situation is impossibly difficult. It's also important to point out that hope, like happiness, is an attitude that can be taught and nurtured.

As a young man, I became interested in prisoner-of-war (POW) stories, particularly those about POW escapes during World War II. The movie, "The Great Escape" with Steve McQueen, typifies this genre. The books and movies I consumed clearly demonstrated the characteristic of hope among the POWs.

When reading about POWs in the Korean War, the authors all described how some prisoners became despondent because escape was significantly more difficult in the Korean environment.

But then I noticed a common observation and conclusion. In cases where POWs gave up hope, they simply turned their heads to the wall and died within a few days. Those who held on to some hope of release kept on living.

The importance of hope was brought home for me personally in my time as a Navy SEAL. You may recall earlier that I mentioned one of my best friends, Bubba Brewton, who was also assigned to SEAL Team Two. We arrived on the same day and attended Army Ranger School together. Following all our training, we were assigned to separate SEAL platoons and began deployments to Vietnam.

During his second SEAL combat deployment period in Vietnam, Bubba was shot six times while on a patrol. His teammates rescued him at great personal risk to themselves, and they moved him to a spot where a MEDEVAC helicopter could pick him up and transfer him to a field hospital.

Unfortunately, the doctors at the field hospital didn't accurately count the bullet entry wounds with the bullet exit wounds, and they inadvertently left one bullet inside him. Sepsis set in, and Bubba quickly started a physical decline.

At first, his attitude toward recovery was good. The doctors had to amputate one leg below the knee in the first surgery. In the second surgery, they took off more of the leg above the knee. Then the third surgery involved removing the rest of the leg and part of his hip. That's when the doctors discovered the extra bullet.

When Bubba was told about the additional body parts that would have to be removed, they said the light simply went out of his eyes. He died shortly after that.

Bubba lost hope when he could no longer envision a future for himself, and that extinguished his will to keep fighting.

This loss hit me hard. Bubba was the most charismatic, big-hearted, fun-loving person I knew. He spent an extra year in college at the University of Alabama just to be a male cheerleader for one more football season. From looking at him, he also seemed like the least likely person to be in the military. I guess Bubba got the last laugh when the Navy subsequently named a Knox-class frigate after him: the U.S.S. Brewton.

This was a great reminder to me that part of having hope is accepting that life is all about change. Sometimes those changes are radical. I believe that it is the strength of the "spiritual" leg of our stool that can make the difference in accepting these situations.

Another example of the power of hope came from a fellow Navy officer I met while studying at the University of Oklahoma. Danny was a former combat pilot who had been shot down in Vietnam and spent six years as a POW.

My friend described what kept him alive during the time that he was captured. It was the vision he had of building his dream house when he was released. He said he spent time every day building that house in his mind, board by board and room by room.

When I met him, he was studying architecture—and actually building that dream house.

While hope is central to our well-being as humans, it doesn't have to be overwhelming in scope. Studies now show benefits accrue to people setting goals, no matter how small, and then taking actual steps to reach them. Knowing that hope can be engendered by working at it in various ways is a huge breakthrough. It's not just a "given" which is there or not there.

## Gratitude

As mentioned, one of the best self-help tools available to us is to practice "an attitude of gratitude." Like most personal habits, this one is strengthened by daily practice.

Everyone has something or someone to be thankful for. Make a list, start small, look around and smell the flowers. Do whatever it takes to realize the people and things you truly appreciate. Although life can be hard at times, a spiritual teacher reminded me some years ago that we—all of us—have received enough love in life, or we wouldn't still be alive.

And I'm reminded of the words of the famous German priest and mystic, Meister Eckhart, who said, "If a person's only prayer is 'Thank you,' he has been preached to enough."

***

The pace of your progress on a spiritual journey is less important than the direction, which involves forward momentum. By adopting the characteristics and emotions discussed in this chapter, you'll have a solid foundation to continue on your path toward finding personal meaning and enlightenment.

***Notes:***

1. This material comes from notes I took while reading *The Earthkeeper's Handbook* by Loren Swift, which may now be out of print.
2. John Fowles has written excellent books including *The French Lieutenant's Woman*, *The Collector*, and *The Aristos*, which is the book outlining Fowles' "world view."

3. Many of these comments on the subject of happiness are engendered from a truly excellent book on this subject, *Build the Life You Want*, by Arthur Brooks and Oprah Winfrey. A deeper understanding of the terms "enjoyment, satisfaction, and purpose" are provided in this book. For example, enjoyment is not simply physical pleasure in some action, but involves the ancillary contributing factors which exist to amplify and sustain the feeling past its purely physical aspects.
4. "Facts about Suicide," Center for Disease Control and Prevention, July 2023.
5. Hawkins, David R., M.D., Ph.D., *The Eye of the I,* Veritas Publishing, Arizona, 2001. This book addresses the topic from both scientific and spiritual points of view.
6. A basic starting point for this material is Hicks, Esther and Jerry, *Abraham* and *Ask and It Is Given,* Hay House, Carlsbad, California, 2004.
7. Roberts, ibid., p. 478.
8. The essence of these succinct thoughts on compassion comes largely from a beautiful article titled "Patient Preparations" by Llona Anne Hress in the *Sedona Journal of Emergence*, February 2024.

# CHAPTER 21
# BALANCING MIND, BODY, & SPIRIT

*Some things to remember:*
*You do not have to prepare for life.*
*You do not have to avoid life.*
*You do not have to monitor life.*
*You do not have to solve life.*
*You do not have to fear life.*
*What you seek outside, you already own.*
*The gathering of all experience is only to know the nature of the Love therein.*
*Enjoy the journey. Your return tickets Home are guaranteed.*[1]
**—Pat Rodegast/Emmanuel**

Toward the end of my active-duty time in the Navy, I received orders to assume responsibilities as Commanding Officer of

SEAL Team Six, which has subsequently become famous in books, documentaries, and movies.

Being a front-line SEAL is in some ways similar to being a professional athlete in a contact sport. As a young man, I largely took the physical aspects of my work in stride. Minor wounds and other injuries usually healed cleanly and rapidly. But after spending so many years involved in highly physical activities, the injuries occurred more frequently and took longer to heal.

As time went on, I did begin to experience more than my share of physical accidents and near-accidents, several of which were life-threatening.

During a night training parachute jump, the rip cord of my main parachute jammed and refused to open. I was falling headfirst at well over 100 miles per hour when I finally deployed my reserve parachute. At that moment, I felt the entire right side of my body go into a spasm which did not release upon landing. Though it wasn't permanent, I suffered a hiatal hernia and also couldn't fully stand up straight for several weeks.

While the physical issues were temporary, I realized that each of the three legs of my mind-body-spirit stool were giving me clear messages: It was finally time for me to follow their lead in life in another direction. After giving the matter very serious thought, I decided that my front-line time as a SEAL was over.

## Revisiting the Three-Legged Stool

As I look back on my career and my life, I can clearly identify the times when my metaphorical three-legged stool was balanced and steady—and times when it wasn't. Hindsight is 20/20, as they say. I'm not sure anyone can fully grasp and appreciate "the state of the stool" in real-time, but I hope the insights I have shared in this book will provide you with a way to frame that analysis.

Giving adequate attention to our mind, body, and spirit is, in my opinion, an essential ingredient for living a good life. We can ignore one of the legs temporarily, but not forever. Recognizing that every one of us will feel the emotional scars of trauma at some point in our lives, we owe it to ourselves to invest in strengthening our support stool. That was a critical part of my recovery, and I believe it can apply to every person reading these pages.

As a recap, I'd like to touch on some of the key things to remember about these three pivotal legs.

### *Mind*

We can reap remarkable benefits if we strive to remain open-minded and focused to the greatest extent possible in the present. The goal is to keep our minds from wandering into the problems or issues from the past or those projected in the future. We can take advantage of the positive mental tools available to us, such as meditation and prayer. And we can get great comfort out of the understanding that the notion of the magical approach to life is inherently self-sustaining. It should remind us of the inherent effortlessness that, in a way, underpins our very existence.

When you find that your mind is excessively concerned or anxious about any aspect of your life, remember that you're thinking those thoughts effortlessly. This realization alone can serve as a reminder that the conscious mind does not possess all the necessary information. It only requires the faith that the means are available, even if those means transcend its own scope.

Great wisdom on this subject comes through Seth's teachings, which is paraphrased here:

> *You are always aware of your actions, even when you may not be consciously aware. Just as your eye knows it can see, even though it cannot directly see itself without the aid of reflection, the world as you perceive it is a reflection of your inner self, not in a literal mirror but in three-dimensional reality. Your thoughts, emotions, and expectations are projected outward, and then you perceive them as the external reality. When it appears that others are observing you, you are, in fact, observing yourself through the lens of your own projections. This principle applies to every facet of your life, both before and after your earthly existence. In a truly astonishing manner, you possess the gift of creating your own experiences.*[2]

### *Body*

Our bodies are simply our souls in flesh. They don't need to be scourged or ignored or mistreated as a lesser part of our being than our spirit. Our bodies are necessary vessels for our existence on earth, and they should be treated with care and love. Enlightenment can only come through the body, not in defiance of it.

Jane Roberts/Seth again provide excellent advice that we should keep in mind:

> *"Philosophies that teach denial of the flesh must ultimately end up preaching a denial of the self, and building contempt for it, because even though the soul is couched in muscle and bone, it is meant to experience that reality, not refute it."*[3]

### *Spirit*

We now understand that our spiritual urge for connection and understanding is innate in every human being. This inner desire also needs to be treated like a physical muscle that should be exercised and consciously strengthened as we go through life. Spirit grows and supports us with a focus on it, but withers if ignored.

With regard to God or "All That Is," we should live with an attitude of reverence and awe, and not in slavish fear of judgment. Everything has a reason to be, and to be who or what it is.

As so aptly put by jazz singer Ethel Waters:

*"God does not make junk."*

It seems time for us to outgrow old myths of both science and religion. We are not born in "original sin." We are not accidental happenings at the end of a long chain of gene-eat-gene, cell-eat-cell, and species-eat-species that follows a murderous chain of survival of the fittest. Our world is created from within, sustained from within, and driven by the value fulfillment of everything in it, by love and desire, and by inner cooperative exuberance.[4]

Accepting the life we have is a mature spiritual step on the road to opening to the greater part of ourselves. This provides help in learning from our current situations and creating more positive results in our lives.

Mary Margaret Moore is clear about expanding our understanding of God:

*"God is everything. Nothing is separate from God. God is the yearning to have an empowered way of being in the world so that one feels one is doing what one wants to do... Hear this deeply: whatever you yearn for, whatever face it is taking, it is God."*[5]

And as the famous Sufi mystic Rumi teaches:

*"What you are seeking is seeking you."*

Finally, I will quote author and channel Miriandra Rota, who is another of my favorite teachers:

> *"The purpose of physicality is to experience awakening while incarnate – awakening to truth, awakening to the truth of who you really are, and perhaps more so, awakening to the totality of being, which is letting go of the illusion of separation from the whole."*[6]

Understanding the bigger implications of our three-legged stool and the metaphysical tenets I have summarized can be a true blessing and a lifelong, loving support system for those inclined to explore them. Actively incorporating these materials into your life can give you a harmonious method of analyzing events and promote a higher quality of living. It can put you back in touch with the magical feelings of being the child that you were and provide a positive support base for your journey.

## Finding Our Purpose

We are blessed to live in an age where, in many places, we have the freedom to express independent spiritual thoughts and follow those quests without fear of reprisals or being ostracized by a religion or society. We can go beyond the teachings of any one religious dogma if we feel led to do so by our minds and hearts. We simply need to begin by having a desire to learn and to be our best selves. Our individual paths can remain open to experience with both intellect and intuition as guides.

The central purpose of each life is to be—a task we can't ultimately fail since *we exist.* Beyond that, we must remain open to sensing our other purposes in moments of deep peace and joy. This direct cognition is available to all of us, but only if we are proactive about looking for it.

Dare to open your mind to the idea that a personal spiritual search is a fundamental support in your life journey. If you don't go looking for something when you've lost it, you will rarely find it. The presence of God is not to be found only in heaven, but also here on earth.

That concept is reflected beautifully in two words you've probably heard before. But the next time you hear them, I hope the deeper meaning will speak to you in a fresh way.

> ***Aloha*** is an ancient Hawaiian greeting which originally means, "The God light in me recognizes the God light in you, in this now moment."

> ***Namaste*** is an ancient greeting in India that shows the utmost respect, meaning, "I bow to the God in you."

I hope the pages in this book have given you a glimpse of the radical importance of your spiritual journey for finding meaning in life and balancing your mind-body-spirit support system—particularly when you've been through difficult times. The concepts here played an extraordinary role in helping me move "beyond the Trident." As we open to the realization that we can expand our understanding and awareness of ourselves, we can begin to view even the most tragic events as having a deeper purpose and meaning for our lives.

If you're intrigued by anything in this book, I encourage you to follow your curiosity. Find out more about the topics and the teachers you've read about. It could be a mind-opening, life-altering experience.

## Moving Ahead

During my final semester at the Naval Academy, I took a voluntary course in advanced Spanish literature. The class was taught by a Spaniard professor named Santiago de Los Mozos Mocha. We referred to him as "Don" Santiago.

He was barely five feet tall and a truly elegant dresser, like the men of all social and economic levels in Spain at that time. He had spent several years as a POW during the Spanish Civil War, and he was lucky to have lived through that truly horrendous experience.

He was the most impressive professor I ever had. A primary requirement for his course was to memorize two verses by famous Spaniards—messages that he told us kept him alive during his time in captivity. I want to end this book with one of those, which is from the Carmelite nun and prominent Spanish mystic, Saint Teresa:

**Nada te turbe**
**Nada te espante**
**Todo se pasa**
**Dios no se muda**
**Con paciencia todo se alcanza**
**El que a Dios tiene, nada le falta**
**Dios solo basta.**

Which translates to:

**Let nothing disturb you**
**Let nothing scare you**
**Everything passes by**
**God is unchanging**
**With patience everything is gained**
**He who has God, lacks nothing**
**God alone is sufficient.**

You already have all you need to live your life to the fullest. You only need to uncover it.

I wish you all the best on your journey.

*Aloha* and *Namaste.*

**Notes:**

1. Rodegast, Pat, and Stanton, Judith, *Emmanuel's Book III*, Bantam Books, New York, p. ix.
2. This paragraph is a paraphrased version of Seth. Roberts, *Dreams (Volume II),* op. cit., p. 470.
3. Roberts, Jane, *The Nature of Personal Reality*, op. cit., p. 235.
4. "Value fulfillment" means that each form of life seeks toward the fulfillment and unfolding of all the capacities that it senses within the living framework of its existence, knowing that the individual fulfillment and unfolding of each other species of life is also benefitted. The Seth material discusses the concept in depth in various books, and a pondering of its importance is revelatory in itself.
5. Moore, Mary-Margaret, *Bartholomew—Planetary Brother*, p. 63.
6. Rota, Miriandra, *Sedona Journal of Emergency*, March 2017, p. 40.

# POSTSCRIPT

I turned 80 in 2023. My wife Heather and I live in Austin, Texas, where I am known as the neighborhood "dog whisperer." Every day, I have a changing cadre of neighbors' dogs that I exercise and then feed them a "full English breakfast." I get as much pleasure out of this activity as the dogs do.

I am still focused on the strength and balance of the three mind-body-spirit legs of the stool that support me. I begin each day with some spiritual reading and a short meditation. My exercise comes from living in a neighborhood called "Great Hills," where I do my morning walk/jog with the dogs daily. Three days each week, I do circuit weight training, followed by simple yoga and core-strengthening mat work. Heather monitors what we eat to keep it healthy.

A priority goal in my life now is to be of service, both to myself and to others in whatever small ways present themselves. There are still "two dogs" living in my mind. I make a daily conscious effort to feed the loving one.

Although I'm officially retired, I helped found a 501(c)(3) charity in 2020 called the *Personal Excellence Foundation* (PEF). This organization has a mind-body-spirit focus for "tweens" and teens, primarily ages 10 to 14. Anyone paying attention realizes that adolescents worldwide are feeling the increased stresses of the issues and conflicts of our modern world, and many now need specialized help to address behavioral mental-health issues.

We initially developed PEF kits to assist parents, caregivers, and therapists in opening and/or broadening conversations with young people about the importance of the three-legged stool. These discussions come at a critical point in their lives, when they are beginning to ask the bigger questions about themselves and life—and are most receptive to increasing their understanding. With the advent of the COVID pandemic and the shut-down of most young persons' meeting venues, we shifted focus to put this material online.

In 2021, we founded a new company called *Lucero Speaks,* which allowed us to "gamify" the PEF subject matter for the same audience and purpose. The Lucero app is a therapeutic game that adolescents play, and it takes them on a journey toward self-understanding and improvement. It is focused on strengthening the mental health of young users while being positively engaging and fun.

The Lucero app is now available through the Apple Store and Google Play. (www.lucerospeaks.com)

I have written this book with the hope that it will prove useful to others and to say "Thank You" to God/Source/All That Is for all of my life's experiences.

If you have found anything interesting or useful in this book, please leave a short book review on Amazon. Since this book is self-published, a major tool Amazon will use in deciding whether to promote this book or not will be the number and quality of book reviews left on the Amazon landing page for this book. I will read every review and make improvements to the book accordingly.

Should anyone wish to contact me personally, please email me directly at tom.murphy@beyondthetrident.com

## The God Who Only Knows Four Words

*Every*
*Child*
*Has known God,*

*Not the God of names,*
*Not the God of don'ts,*
*Not the God who ever does*
*Anything weird,*

*But the God who only knows four words,*
*And keeps repeating them, saying:*

*"Come dance with Me."*

*Come*

*Dance*

**—Hafiz, *The Gift***

# APPENDIX

In this section, you'll find an Alphabetical List of Resources, as well as some reading selections by category. These lists extend beyond the scope of references you'll find in the book. They include a broader range of sources which have influenced me over the years—ones I believe are all worthy of being read by others.

I wish it were possible to highlight the import of every single resource found on these lists. I have attempted to do this for many of them throughout the chapters and the notes at the end, but each one has extraordinary impact.

I don't think anyone can read the Jane Roberts/Seth series of books in any depth without an expanded understanding of the magnificent scope of what it means to be a human being, and changing their thoughts about the nature of reality. No one can read *There Is a River* about Edgar Cayce by Thomas Sugrue and not be astounded by the life and extraordinary medical and metaphysical abilities of that man. And Ken Wilber's *No Boundary* will undoubtedly prompt people to reassess their human capabilities to touch mystical states of mind.

For those of you are new to metaphysics, I encourage you to start with *Emmanuel's Book* by Pat Rodegast. Let this simple, loving wisdom sink in and then see where it leads you.

## Alphabetical List of References


- Bailey, Alice A., *A Treatise on Cosmic Fire*, Lucis Publishing Company, 1925.
- Barks, Coleman, and Moyne, John, Translators, *The Essential Rumi*, Harper, San Francisco, 2004.
- Bartholomew, Mary-Margaret Moore, *I Come as a Brother*, Hay House, Inc., Carlsbad, California, 1984.
- Beck, Martha, *The Way of Integrity*, Penguin Life, 2021.
- Berger, Barbara, *Gateway to Grace*, Beamteam Books, Copenhagen, Denmark, 1997.
- Bro, Harmon, Ph.D., and Cayce, Hugh Lynn, *Edgar Cayce on Dreams*, Warner Books, 1988.
- Brooks, Arthur, and Winfrey, Oprah, *Build the Life You Want*, Portfolio Penguin, New York, 2023.
- Bryson, Bill, *The Body: A Guide for Occupants*, Random House, New York, 2019.
- Burns, Barbara, *Channeling: Evolutionary Exercises for Channels,* Light Technology Publishing, 1993.
- Caddy, Eileen, *God Spoke to Me,* Findhorn Press, Scotland, 1971.
- Campbell, Joseph, *The Hero's Journey*, Random House, New York, multiple years.
- Castaneda, Carlos, *Journey to Ixtlan*, Washington Square Press, New York, 1962.
- Cayce, Hugh Lynn (ed.), *The Edgar Cayce Collection*, Bonanza Books, New York, 1969.

- Chapman, Cathy, Ph.D., *Trauma and PTSD*, Light Technology Publishing, Flagstaff, Arizona, 2020.
- Chopra, Deepak, *The Seven Spiritual Laws of Success* and *Ageless Body, Timeless Mind*, Harmony Publishing, multiple years.
- Copra, Fritz, *The Tao of Physics*, Shambhala Press, 2010.
- Crookall, Robert, *Out of the Body Experiences*, Citadel Press, New Jersey, 1970.
- Elie, Paul, *The Life You Save May Be Your Own: An American Pilgrimage,* Farrar, Straus, and Girard, 2004.
- Ferris, Timothy, *The 4-Hour Work Week*, Harmony, 2004.
- Fowles, John, *The Aristos*, Little, Brown and Co., Boston, 1964.
- Gibran, Khalil, *The Prophet*, Fingerprint Publishing, 2018.
- Hawkins, David R., M.D., Ph.D., *The Eye of the I,* Veritas Publishing, Arizona, 2001.
- Hafiz (translated by D. Ladinsky), *The Gift,* Penguin Compass, New York, 1999.
- Hicks, Esther and Jerry, *Abraham, Ask and It Is Given,* Hay House, Carlsbad, California, 2004.
- Jung, Carl, *Memories, Dreams and Reflections,* Vintage, 1989.
- Keith, Thomas H., and Riebling, J. Terry, *SEAL Warrior*, St. Martin's Press, 2009.
- Klimo, Jon, and Tart, Charles, *Channeling,* St. Martin's Press, New York, 1991.
- Kubler-Ross, Elizabeth, *On Death and Dying,* Celestial Arts, 2008.
- McGilchrist, Iain, *The Master and His Emissary*, Yale University Press, 2019.
- Miller, Lisa, Ph.D., *The Spiritual Child* and *The Awakened Brain*, Picador and Random House, New York, multiple years.

- Monroe, Robert, *Journeys Out of the Body*, Doubleday Anchor Press, New York, 1971.
- Moorjani, Anita, *Dying To Be Me*, Hay House, 2002.
- Muldoon, Sylvan, and Carrington, Hereward, *The Projection of the Astral Body,* Rider and Company, London, 1929.
- Pierrakos, Eva, and Thesenga, Donovan, *The Pathwork of Self Transformation,* Bantam, 1990, and *Surrender to God Within*, Pathwork Press, 1997.
- Purcel, Jach, *The Sacred Journey: You and Your Higher Self,* Concept Synergy Publishing, 1987.
- Reed, Henry, and Cayce, Charles Thomas, *Edgar Cayce on Channeling Your Higher Self,* Warner Books, New York, 1989.
- Rinpoche, Sogyal, *The Tibetan Book of Living and Dying,* Random House, London, 2002.
- Roman, Sanaya, and Packer, Duane, *Opening to Channel,* H.J. Kramer, Inc., Tiburon, California, 19
- Roberts, Jane, *Seth Speaks, The Nature of Personal Reality, The Nature of the Psyche: It's Human Expression; The Individual and the Nature of Mass Events, The Unknown Reality (2 Volumes), Dreams, "Evolution," and Value Fulfillment (2 Volumes); Dreams and Projections of Consciousness; The Afterdeath Journal of an American Philosopher (William James); The World View of Paul Cezanne;* Prentiss Hall Press, New York, multiple years.
- Rodegast, Pat, and Stanton, Judith, *Emmanuel's Books, I, II, and III,* Bantam Books, New York, multiple years.
- Saratoga and Telstar/Kirin Baugher, *The Final Elimination of the Source of Fear,* Nova Publications, Albuquerque, New Mexico, 1995.
- Spangler, David, *Blessing,* Penguin, New York, 2001.
- Smith, Adam, *Powers of Mind,* Random House, New York, 1975.

- Smith, Cyprian OSB, *The Way of Paradox,* Darton, Longman and Todd LTD, London, 2007.
- Smith, Susy, *Reincarnation for the Millions*, Sherbourne Press, Inc., 1967.
- Schucman, Helen, and Thetford, William, *A Course in Miracles,* Mill Valley, California, Foundation for Inner Peace, 1992.
- Stella, Tom, *A Faith Worth Believing,* Harper Collins Publishers, New York, 2004.
- Stern, Jess, *Edgar Cayce – The Sleeping Prophet,* Bantam Books, New York, 1967.
- Stern, Jess, *The Search for a Soul: Taylor Caldwell's Psychic Lives,* Fawcett Crest Books, 1974.
- Sugrue, Thomas, *Edgar Cayce There Is a River,* ARE Press, Virginia Beach, Virginia, 1997.
- Suzuki, Shunryu, *Zen Mind, Beginner's Mind,* Weatherhill, New York, 1970.
- Taylor, Jill Bolte, *Whole Brain Living*, Hay House Inc., 2021.
- Tolle, Eckhart, *The Power of Now,* New World Library, 1999.
- Underhill, *Mysticism,* Dover Publications, New York, 2002.
- Varty, Boyd, *The Lion Tracker's Guide to Life,* Harper One, 2019.
- Van Der Kolk, Bessel, Ph.D., *The Body Keeps the Score,* Penguin Books, 2014.
- Williamson, Marianne, *A Return to Love*, Thorsons, 1992.
- Yogananda, Paramahansa, *Autobiography of a Yogi,* Self-Realization Fellowship, Los Angeles, California, 1998.
- Young-Sowers, Meredith Lady, *Agartha*, Stillpoint Publishing, 1984.

***Timeless Wisdom***

- Gibran, Khalil, *The Prophet*, Fingerprint Publishing, 2018.
- Hafiz (translated by Daniel Ladinsky), *The Gift,* Penguin Compass, New York, 1999.
- Lao Tzu (translated by John C.H. Wu), *Tao Teh Ching,* Barnes and Noble Press, 1997.

***Young Persons' Books***

- Roberts, Jane, *The Education of Oversoul Seven, The Further Education of Oversoul Seven, Oversoul Seven and the Museum of Time, Emir's Education in the Proper Use of Magical Powers,* multiple publishers and years.
- Hicks, Esther and Jerry, *Sara Book 1, Sara Book 2, Sara Book 3,* Hay House, multiple years.

***Channeling***

- Burns, Barbara, *Channeling: Evolutionary Exercises for Channels,* Light Technology Publishing, 1993.
- Klimo, Jon, and Tart, Charles, *Channeling,* St. Martin's Press, New York, 1991.
- Roberts, Jane, *Psychic Politics*, Prentice Hall, New York, 1976.
- Roman, Sanaya, and Packer, Duane, *Opening to Channel,* H.J. Kramer, Inc., Tiburon, California, 1993.
- Stern, Jess, *Edgar Cayce – The Sleeping Prophet,* Bantam Books, New York, 1967.
- Sugrue, Thomas, *Edgar Cayce "There Is a River,"* ARE Press, Virginia Beach, Virginia, 1997.

### *Dreams and OOBEs*


- Bro, Harmon, Ph.D., and Cayce, Hugh Lynn, *Edgar Cayce on Dreams*, Warner Books, 1988.
- Castaneda, Carlos, *Journey to Ixtlan,* Washington Square Press, New York, 1962.
- Crookall, Robert, *Out of the Body Experiences*, Citadel Press, New Jersey, 1970.
- Jung, Carl, *Memories, Dreams and Reflections,* Vintage, 1989.
- Monroe, Robert, *Journeys Out of the Body,* Doubleday Anchor Press, New York, 1971.
- Muldoon, Sylvan, and Carrington, Hereward, *The Projection of the Astral Body,* Rider and Company, London, 1929.
- Roberts, Jane, *The Nature of the Psyche: Its Human Expression; Dreams, "Evolution," and Value Fulfillment (2 Volumes); Dreams and Projections of Consciousness,* Amber-Allen Press, California, multiple years.
- Van Over, Raymond, *Psychology and Extrasensory Perception*, The New American Library, New York, 1972.


### *Mysticism*


- Hawkins, David R., M.D., Ph.D., *The Eye of the I,* Veritas Publishing, Arizona, 2001.
- Smith, Cyprian OSB, *The Way of Paradox,* Darton, Longman and Todd LTD, London, 2007.
- Underhill, Evelyn, *Mysticism,* Dover Publications, New York, 2002.
- Wilber, Ken, *No Boundary* and *The Spectrum of Consciousness*, Quest Books, Wheaton, Illinois, multiple years.

### *Self Help*


- Beck, Martha, *The Way of Integrity*, Penguin Life, 2021.
- Brooks, Arthur, and Winfrey, Oprah, *Build the Life You Want,* Portfolio Penguin, New York, 2023.
- Ferris, Timothy, *The 4-Hour Work Week,* Harmony, 2004.
- Varty, Boyd, *The Lion Tracker's Guide to Life,* Harper One, 2019.
- Williamson, Marianne, *A Return to Love*, Thorsons Publishers, 1992.

# ABOUT THE AUTHOR

Tom has over 40 years of experience managing both government and commercial organizations, and has served as President/CEO and Director of International Business Development of four separate public and private companies in the Construction, Computer Software and Biotechnology fields.

Tom is a retired Navy Captain, a combat veteran, an Olmsted Scholar, and served as a U.S. Navy SEAL for 25 years, rising through the ranks to become Commanding Officer of two different Navy SEAL commands, including the much-publicized SEAL Team Six. He also worked directly for Chief of Naval Operations, where he assisted in the creation of the U.S. Navy's Personal Excellence Program. This program was developed to link the Navy's multiple remedial programs into a broader framework of understanding of the importance of a combined holistic approach to helping sailors improve themselves. While on active duty in the U.S. Navy, he also served on the Board of Directors of the George and Carol Olmsted Foundation, placing scholars in universities world-wide.

He is a graduate of the U.S. Naval Academy and received his M.A. in International Relations and Ph.D. in Political Science from the University of Oklahoma as an Olmsted Scholar. Tom and his wife Heather are both retired and live in Austin, Texas.

To contact Tom:
tom.murphy@beyondthetrident.com

Made in the USA
Las Vegas, NV
09 December 2024